THE OLD
FARMER'S AL.
FOR
KIDS

VOLUME 10

YANKEE PUBLISHING INCORPORATED

A 100% Employee-Owned Company

THE OLD FARMER'S ALMANAC BOOKS

Publisher: Sherin Pierce
Editor in Chief: Janice Stillman
Creative Director: Colleen Quinnell
Series Editor: Sarah Perreault
Managing Editor: Jack Burnett
Senior Editor: Heidi Stonehill
Associate Editor: Tim Goodwin
Contributors: Mel Allen, Bob Berman, Sarah Bond, Alice Cary, Renee Dobbs, Mare-Anne Jarvela, Rosemary Mosco, Sheryl Normandeau, Jack Singal, Robin Sweetser, Jen Wooster-McBride

V.P., New Media and Production: Paul Belliveau
Production Director: David Ziarnowski
Production Manager: Brian Johnson
Senior Production Artists: Jennifer Freeman, Rachel Kipka, Janet Selle

Companion Web site: Almanac.com/Kids

Senior Digital Editor: Catherine Boeckmann
Senior Web Designer: Amy O'Brien
Digital Marketing Specialists: Jessica Garcia, Holly Sanderson
E-mail Marketing Specialist: Eric Bailey
E-commerce Marketing Director: Alan Henning
Programming: Reinvented, Inc.

For additional information about this and other publications from *The Old Farmer's Almanac,* visit **Almanac.com** or call **1-800-ALMANAC (1-800-256-2622)**

Distributed in the book trade in the United States by HarperCollins Publishers and in Canada by Firefly Books Ltd.

Direct-to-retail and bulk sales are handled by Stacey Korpi, 800-895-9265, ext. 160

Yankee Publishing Inc., P.O. Box 520, 1121 Main Street, Dublin, New Hampshire 03444

ISBN: 978-1-57198-959-8

ISSN: 1948-061X

FIRST PRINTING OF VOLUME 10

Thank you to everyone who had a hand in producing this Almanac and getting it to market, including printers, distributors, and sales and delivery people, and thanks to all of you who bought it!

HEY, YOU!

YES, YOU!

DID YOU KNOW THAT THIS *OLD FARMER'S ALMANAC FOR KIDS* HAS ITS OWN WEB SITE?

NIGHT SKY	JOKES & FUN	TIME TRAVEL	ANIMAL LOVERS	WEATHER WATCH

That's right! **ALMANAC.COM/KIDS** is filled with **TONS MORE** of the same cool, quirky, awesome, and amazing stuff that you see on these pages!

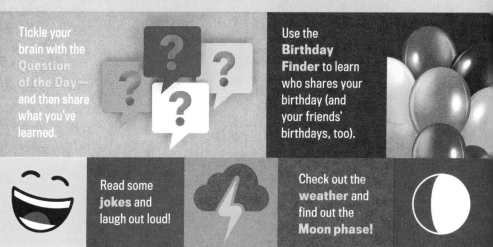

Tickle your brain with the **Question of the Day** — and then share what you've learned.

Use the **Birthday Finder** to learn who shares your birthday (and your friends' birthdays, too).

Read some **jokes** and laugh out loud!

Check out the **weather** and find out the **Moon phase!**

Explore to find more incredible stuff! Most important, have fun!

EXPAND YOUR EXPERIENCE AT
ALMANAC.COM/KIDS

CONTENTS

8

30

42

ON THE FARM

NATURE

58

76

106

90

CONTENTS

118

AWESOME ACHIEVERS

FOOD

SPORTS

HEALTH

126

144

152

AMUSEMENT

158

FUN & GAMES

162

123

WHAT HAPPENED IN HISTORY?

JANUARY

Convert to metric on p. 170

2
On this day in 2010, a numerically rare event occurred: The numbers in its date, 01-02-2010, read the same forward and backward.

4
7.5-magnitude earthquake struck off coast of Alaska, 2013

5
Television dancing judge Carrie Ann Inaba born, 1968

7
Snow covered Sahara Desert in Aïn Sefra, Algeria, 2018

*Little January
Tapped at my door today.
And said, "Put on your winter wraps,
And come outdoors to play."*
–Winifred C. Marshall, American writer (1761–1839)

9
Apple Inc. introduced first iPhone, 2007

13
Actress Julia Louis-Dreyfus born, 1961

14
Rare black rhino born at St. Louis Zoo, Missouri, 2011

18
Actor Karan Brar born, 1999

21
National Granola Bar Day

22
Roberta Bondar became first Canadian woman in space, 1992

24
Patent for microwave oven granted, 1950

26
Rocky Mountain National Park established, Colorado, 1915

29
Singer Adam Lambert born, 1982

30
Buffalo escaped from South Dakota auction and ended up in Rapid City department store dressing room, 2005

31
Baseball player Jackie Robinson born, 1919

MOON NAME: FULL WOLF MOON

FEBRUARY

MOON NAME: FULL SNOW MOON

1
Ice storm produced layer of ice up to 4 inches thick from Texas to Pennsylvania, 1951

2
Singer Shakira born, 1977

4
Olympic gymnast Carly Patterson born, 1988

6
34th U.S. president Dwight D. Eisenhower shot hole-in-one, 1968

7
Ellen MacArthur set new world record by sailing around the world in 71 days, 14 hours, 18 minutes, and 33 seconds, 2005

9
Actor Michael B. Jordan born, 1987

11
Opening day of first Canada Winter Games, Quebec City, 1967

14
YouTube founded, 2005

17
Musician Ed Sheeran born, 1991

21
Washington Monument dedicated, Washington, D.C., 1885

23
Actress Dakota Fanning born, 1994

25
Storm dropped 49.3 inches of snow on Mt. Washington, New Hampshire, 1969

27
National Strawberry Day

28
Performer Natasha Veruschka "swallowed" 22.83-inch sword, 2009

*Come when the rains
Have glazed the snow and clothed the trees with ice,
While the slant sun of February pours
Into the bowers a flood of light.*
–William Cullen Bryant, American poet (1794–1878)

CALENDAR

MARCH

1
Actress Lupita Nyong'o born, 1983

*It is the first mild day of March:
Each minute sweeter than before
The redbreast sings from
the tall larch
That stands beside our door.*
–William Wordsworth,
English poet (1770–1850)

24
National Chocolate-Covered Raisins Day

3
Steve Fossett became first person to fly around the world solo without stopping or refueling, 2005

4
Abraham Lincoln inaugurated as the 16th U.S. president, 1861

6
City of Toronto, Canada, incorporated, 1834

7
Phil Mahre won third consecutive alpine skiing World Cup championship, 1983

9
Olympic gymnast Suni Lee born, 2003

13
Planet Uranus discovered by Sir William Herschel, 1781

14
Basketball player Steph Curry born, 1988

17
University of California (Berkeley) announced development of californium, a new element, 1950

19
5.38-inch-wide, 9.8-ounce hailstone fell in Walter, Alabama, 2018

20
Hockey player Bobby Orr born, 1948

23
NASA astronaut John Young smuggled corned beef sandwich aboard *Gemini 3*, 1965

26
First female U.S. Supreme Court justice Sandra Day O'Connor born, 1930

28
22 tornadoes spotted in the Carolinas, 1984

31
Daylight Saving Time went into effect, 1918

MOON NAME: FULL WORM MOON

APRIL

MOON NAME: FULL PINK MOON

1
Acrobat Willy Martignon broke world record for longest-distance somersaulting slam dunk, 2007

2
Wind gust of 199.5 mph at Cannon Mountain, New Hampshire, 1973

4
First totally artificial heart implanted into human, 1969

6
Jimmy Dewar invented cream-filled sponge cake now known as the Twinkie, 1930

7
Booker T. Washington became first Black on U.S. postage stamp, 1940

9
Rapper Lil Nas X born, 1999

11
Apollo 13 launched, 1970

12
Author Beverly Cleary born, 1916

13
National Peach Cobbler Day

15
Actress Emma Watson born, 1990

18
Beauty and the Beast, first Broadway musical based on Disney animated film, opened, 1994

19
Women granted right to vote in Alberta, Canada, 1916

22
Earth Day celebrated for first time in U.S., 1970

23
Actor Dev Patel born, 1990

25
Buddy, first guide dog for the blind in the U.S., was teamed up with his owner, Morris S. Frank, 1928

30
George Washington inaugurated as 1st U.S. president, 1789

The wild and windy March once more
Has shut his gates of sleet,
And given us back the April-time,
So fickle and so sweet.

–Alice Cary, American poet (1820–71)

MAY

The flowers in the breeze are swaying, swaying,
The whole wide world is out a-Maying.
–Genevieve Mary Irons, English hymnist (1855–1928)

2
Soccer player David Beckham born, 1975

3
Dale Davis, legally blind 78-year-old bowler from Iowa, recorded perfect game during league play, 2008

5
Pablo Picasso's *Boy With a Pipe* sold at auction for $104,168,000, 2004

6
Baseball player Willie Mays born, 1931

8
Coca-Cola went on sale, 1886

9
Actress Rosario Dawson born, 1979

11
Dust storms darkened skies from Oklahoma to Atlantic Ocean, 1934

14
4-year-old Louis Dieudonné became King Louis XIV of France, 1643

16
Discovery of 2.6 billion-year-old water found in Ontario mine announced, 2013

18
Actress Tina Fey born, 1970

19
Boston Red Sox pitcher Jon Lester threw no-hitter against Kansas City Royals, 2008

20
680-pound goliath grouper caught off Fernandina Beach, Florida, 1961

21
BTS received "Top Social Artist" award at the *Billboard* Music Awards, 2017

23
Benjamin Franklin created own pair of bifocals, 1785

25
Star Wars released in theaters, 1977

28
Actor Cameron Boyce born, 1999

29
National Biscuit Day

MOON NAME: FULL FLOWER MOON

JUNE

MOON NAME: FULL STRAWBERRY MOON

1
Model Heidi Klum born, 1973

3
Sally Jane Priesand became first American female ordained as rabbi, 1972

6
George Harbo and Frank Samuelsen began 55-day row across Atlantic, 1896

7
Musician Prince born, 1958

8
For first time in 121.5 years, Sun partially eclipsed by Venus, 2004

9
Actor Adamo Ruggiero born, 1986

10
National Iced Tea Day

13
Snowplows needed to clean up softball-size hailstones, Denver, Colorado, 1984

14
Cows gathered around just-fallen meteorite fragment, St. Robert, Quebec, 1994

*June's a month, and June's a name,
Never yet hath had its fame.
Summer's in the sound of June,
Summer and a deepened tune.*
–Leigh Hunt, English poet (1784–1859)

19
First Father's Day celebrated, Spokane, Washington, 1910

20
Actress Nicole Kidman born, 1967

21
Ferris wheel debuted at World's Columbian Exposition, Chicago, Illinois, 1893

23
Olympic sprinter Wilma Rudolph born, 1940

24
John Isner of the U.S. defeated Nicolas Mahut of France at Wimbledon in longest tennis match to date (11 hours, 5 minutes), 2010

26
John Tyler became first U.S. president to marry while in office, 1844

27
Fashion designer Vera Wang born, 1949

30
Leap second added to world's atomic clocks to keep up with slowing rotation of Earth, 2012

JULY

When the heat like a mist veil floats,
And poppies flame in the rye,
And the silver note in the streamlet's throat
Has softened almost to a sigh,
It is July.

–Susan Hartley Swett, American poet (1843–1907)

1
John A. Macdonald became first prime minister of Canada, 1867

4
U.S. minister to France presented with Statue of Liberty, Paris, France, 1884

6
Hailstone measuring 5.5 inches in diameter and weighing 1.5 pounds fell, Potter, Nebraska, 1928

7
Figure skater Michelle Kwan born, 1980

9
Jim Purol set Guinness World Record for "Most Seats Sat On in 48 Hours" by sitting in 39,250 stadium seats, 2008

11
National Blueberry Muffin Day

13
Actor Harrison Ford born, 1942

14
75-foot snow pile from previous winter finally melted, Boston, Massachusetts, 2015

18
Hockey player Jamie Benn born, 1989

20
First International Special Olympics held, Chicago, Illinois, 1968

23
Bluegrass/country musician Alison Krauss born, 1971

24
9-year-old Emma Houlston became youngest person to pilot plane across Canada, 1988

26
Actress Sandra Bullock born, 1964

30
Actor Laurence Fishburne born, 1961

31
Astronauts David Scott and James Irwin became first to drive vehicle on Moon, 1971

MOON NAME: FULL BUCK MOON

AUGUST

MOON NAME: FULL STURGEON MOON

1
Actor Jason Momoa born, 1979

3
National Watermelon Day

4
Thomas Stevens became first to bicycle across U.S., 1884

5
Actress Olivia Holt born, 1997

7
Peace Bridge, between Buffalo, New York, and Fort Erie, Ontario, dedicated, 1927

8
Musician Shawn Mendes born, 1998

10
Ruth Bader Ginsburg sworn in as justice of U.S. Supreme Court, 1993

12
13-year-old Marjorie Gestring won Olympic gold medal for springboard diving, 1936

14
Actress Halle Berry born, 1966

15
Ignacio Anaya García, inventor of nachos, born, 1895

17
Swimmer Michael Phelps became first person to win eight gold medals in single Olympics, 2008

19
72-pound lake trout caught in Great Bear Lake, Northwest Territories, 1995

20
Salt crystals fell from the sky over Switzerland, 1870

23
Basketball player Kobe Bryant born, 1978

24
Cornelius Swartwout patented waffle iron, 1869

28
Dr. Martin Luther King Jr. delivered "I Have a Dream" speech, 1963

30
Houston Comets won WNBA championship in league's first season, 1997

All Nature helps to swell the song
And chant the same refrain;
July and June have slipped away
And August's here again.
—Helen Maria Winslow, American writer (1851–1938)

SEPTEMBER

September strews the woodlot o'er
With many a brilliant color;
The world is brighter than before,
Why should our hearts be duller?
–Thomas W. Parsons, American poet (1819–92)

1
Actress Zendaya born, 1996

4
127-pound cabbage won a prize at Alaska State Fair, 2009

5
Football player Mac Jones born, 1998

6
Mayflower set sail from Plymouth, England, 1620

8
Singer P!nk born, 1979

9
Queen Elizabeth II became longest-reigning monarch in British history, 2015

12
Hong Kong Disneyland opened, 2005

13
Chocolatier Milton Hershey born, 1857

14
Crayola announced new crayon color "Bluetiful," 2017

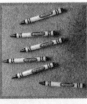

16
People reported seeing lake monster Ogopogo in Okanagan Lake, British Columbia, 1926

17
Racecar driver Jimmie Johnson born, 1975

18
George Meegan finished almost 7-year-long walk from tip of South America to Prudhoe Bay, Alaska, 1983

20
Peoria, Illinois, had first summer freeze on record, 1991

23
Planet Neptune discovered, 1846

25
National Quesadilla Day

26
Prairie View A&M University football team snapped 80-game losing streak, 1998

28
437 people dressed as Superman set world record, Calgary, Alberta, 2001

30
John Lennon honored with star on Hollywood Walk of Fame, 1988

MOON NAME: FULL CORN MOON

OCTOBER

MOON NAME: FULL HUNTER'S MOON

2
Peanuts cartoon made debut, 1950

3
Singer Gwen Stefani born, 1969

6
Ucluelet Brynnor Mines, British Columbia, recorded 19.26 inches of rain in 24 hours, 1967

7
Georgia Tech defeated Cumberland University in football 222-0, 1916

8
New York Yankees pitcher Don Larsen pitched World Series perfect game, 1956

11
Golfer Michelle Wie West born, 1989

14
Actress Rowan Blanchard born, 2001

16
Copyright for melody of "Happy Birthday to You" registered, 1893

17
Mother Teresa awarded Nobel Peace Prize, 1979

18
Alaska transferred from Russia to U.S., 1867

21
The Guggenheim Museum of Art opened in New York City, 1959

22
Kwanzaa U.S. postage stamp first issued, 1997

23
Actor Ryan Reynolds born, 1976

26
2,000-pound, 8-foot-long cannon belonging to pirate Blackbeard removed from waters near Beaufort, North Carolina, 2011

27
DuPont announced invention of nylon, 1938

28
National Chocolate Day

29
Hurricane Ginny left 13 inches of snow on Aroostook County, Maine, 1963

31
Drilling completed on Mount Rushmore, South Dakota, 1941

The mug of cider simmered slow,
The apples sputtered in a row,
And close at hand the basket stood
With nuts from brown October's wood.
–John Greenleaf Whittier, American poet (1807–92)

NOVEMBER

November comes
And November goes,
With the last red berries
And the first white snows.

–Elizabeth Coatsworth, American writer (1893–1986)

2
Nik Wallenda set two world records with two high-wire walks between Chicago skyscrapers, 2014

3
John Adams elected 2nd U.S. president, 1796

5
Bronze memorial statue of Mr. Fred Rogers dedicated, Pittsburgh, Pennsylvania, 2009

6
Actress Emma Stone born, 1988

9
29th subtropical storm (Theta) formed in Atlantic, setting new record for most named storms in single season, 2020

11
Vietnam Women's Memorial dedicated, Washington, D.C., 1993

14
Home improvement guru Chip Gaines born, 1974

15
Walt Disney announced plans to build Epcot, 1965

17
Aurora borealis seen throughout U.S., 1835

19
Soccer player Pelé scored 1,000th goal, Maracana Stadium, Rio de Janeiro, Brazil, 1969

21
Snowflakes fell on Orlando, Florida, 2006

22
Humane Society of the United States founded, 1954

25
National Parfait Day

27
Martial artist Bruce Lee born, 1940

28
Future U.S. president Thomas Jefferson recorded in his journal: "It is so cold that the freezing of the ink on the point of my pen renders it difficult to write," 1796

29
Football player Russell Wilson born, 1988

30
Discovery of 215 fossilized pterosaur eggs in Gobi Desert, China, announced, 2017

MOON NAME: FULL BEAVER MOON

DECEMBER

MOON NAME: FULL COLD MOON

1
Black passenger Rosa Parks arrested for refusing to give up bus seat to white rider, Montgomery, Alabama, 1955

2
Singer Charlie Puth born, 1991

4
Matisse's *Le Bateau* rehung after being upside down in The Museum of Modern Art for 47 days, New York City, 1961

5
First six astronauts chosen for Canadian Space Program, 1983

6
Claymation holiday classic *Rudolph the Red-Nosed Reindeer* made television debut, 1964

8
National Brownie Day

9
Twin polar bear cubs born at Hellabrunn Zoo, Munich, Germany, 2013

10
Drummer Meg White born, 1974

12
Orange soil discovered on Moon by *Apollo 17* mission, 1972

13
Musician Taylor Swift born, 1989

15
"Great Blizzard" hit Canadian Prairie provinces, 1964

16
Ice jam closed Ohio River from Warsaw, Kentucky, to Rising Sun, Indiana, 1917

18
Director Steven Spielberg born, 1946

21
Actor Samuel L. Jackson born, 1948

24
CONAD (later NORAD) began to track Santa Claus, 1955

26
Law amended to admit girls into Little League baseball, 1974

27
12.5 inches of snow fell on Dumas, Texas, 2000

28
Actress Maitreyi Ramakrishnan born, 2001

30
Samoa skipped this day in order to move from eastern to western side of International Date Line, 2011

*To the cold December heaven
Came the pale Moon and the stars,
As the yellow Sun was sinking
Behind the purple bars.*
—Charles Dawson Shanly, Irish-born Canadian poet (1811–75)

BIRTHDAY BLING

JANUARY

GARNET
Common color: Red
Symbolizes: Love and friendship
Was once thought to: Provide safe passage on long journeys; protect warriors in battle
Fact: The world's largest garnet mine is located at Barton Mines in New York's Adirondack Mountains.

FEBRUARY

AMETHYST
Common color: Purple
Symbolizes: Calm and clarity
Was once thought to: Bring good luck to those who dreamed of receiving it
Fact: The world's largest amethyst geode, "Empress of Uruguay," stands 11 feet tall and weighs 2.5 tons.

MAY

EMERALD
Common color: Green
Symbolizes: Loyalty and new beginnings
Was once thought to: Reveal the future if placed under the tongue
Fact: Seattle, Washington, is nicknamed the Emerald City.

JUNE

PEARL
Common color: Creamy white
Symbolizes: Purity and modesty
Was once thought to: Come from mermaid tears; provide protection from fire-breathing dragons
Fact: In 1917, Pierre Cartier, a famous jeweler, traded a double-strand pearl necklace for a Fifth Avenue mansion in New York City.

SEPTEMBER

SAPPHIRE
Common color: Blue
Symbolizes: Truth and sincerity
Was once thought to: Foster peace between enemies
Fact: The engagement ring of England's Catherine, Princess of Wales, features a 12-carat sapphire.

OCTOBER

OPAL
Common color: Multicolor with black or white background
Symbolizes: Hope and truth
Was once thought to: Contain the powers of all colored stones
Fact: "Olympic Australis," the most valuable opal, was found in Australia during the 1976 Summer Olympics.

Your birthday is a very special day
of the year, and it can be even brighter
thanks to the precious gem
associated with your birth month.

MARCH

AQUAMARINE

Common color: Blue, blue-green
Symbolizes: Happiness and
eternal youth
Was once thought to: Provide
protection for those traveling on
water; bring good luck while fishing
Fact: Aquamarine is the state
gemstone of Colorado.

APRIL

DIAMOND

Common color: Colorless/clear
Symbolizes: Strength and beauty
Was once thought to: Be formed by
lightning and the tears of gods
Fact: Diamonds are harder than
almost any other naturally occurring
material.

JULY

RUBY

Common color: Red
Symbolizes: Protection and wealth
Was once thought to: Provide
protection in battle; create
invincibility
Fact: In 1960, in Malibu, California,
Theodore Maiman used a synthetic
ruby to construct the first laser.

AUGUST

PERIDOT

Common color: Light green
Symbolizes: Good fortune
and prosperity
Was once thought to: Improve
memory; ward off evil spirits
Fact: Peridots have been found
in meteorites.

NOVEMBER

TOPAZ

Common color: Yellow
Symbolizes: Strength and honor
Was once thought to: Break magic
spells; make wearers invisible
Fact: Naturally colorless and at
times mistaken for diamonds,
topaz stones appear yellow due to
impurities within.

DECEMBER

TURQUOISE

Common color: Blue
Symbolizes: Health and good fortune
Was once thought to: Be found at the
end of a rainbow
Fact: The burial mask of Egyptian
pharaoh King Tut was decorated with
many gems, including turquoise.

A DAY TO HONOR INDIGENOUS PEOPLES

Indigenous Peoples' Day is celebrated
in the United States on the second Monday
in October. In Canada, the holiday is called National
Indigenous Peoples Day and celebrated on June 21.
Indigenous peoples have many customs and traditions
that have been passed down from their ancestors.
Here are a few of the more common practices.

WHAT IT MEANS

INDIGENOUS refers to a group of people who originally lived in a place, rather than people who moved there from somewhere else.

ABORIGINAL refers to groups of people who first inhabited the land and lived in a region from the beginning. "Aboriginal" is usually used to refer to indigenous peoples of Canada and Australia.

FIRST NATIONS refers to indigenous peoples in Canada who are not Inuit (indigenous peoples of the arctic and subarctic regions) or Métis (indigenous peoples of Alberta, Saskatchewan, and Manitoba, as well as parts of British Columbia, Ontario, and the Northwest Territories).

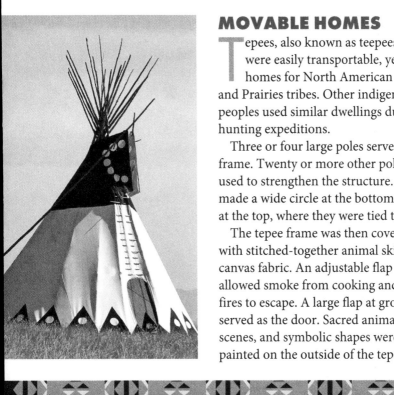

MOVABLE HOMES

Tepees, also known as teepees or tipis, were easily transportable, year-round homes for North American Plains and Prairies tribes. Other indigenous peoples used similar dwellings during hunting expeditions.

Three or four large poles served as the frame. Twenty or more other poles were used to strengthen the structure. The poles made a wide circle at the bottom and met at the top, where they were tied together.

The tepee frame was then covered with stitched-together animal skins or canvas fabric. An adjustable flap at the top allowed smoke from cooking and heating fires to escape. A large flap at ground level served as the door. Sacred animals, battle scenes, and symbolic shapes were often painted on the outside of the tepees.

BY THE NUMBERS

As of 2020, there were 574 federally recognized indigenous tribes in the United States, across 36 states. Canada has more then 600 First Nations communities, with more than 1.6 million people in the country identifying as aboriginal.

A TALL TALE

A totem is a natural object, animal, or spirit being that serves as a symbol of a group of people. Totem poles were made by indigenous peoples on the northwest coast of the United States and Canada. Traditionally carved out of red or yellow cedar and often painted with bright colors, totem poles are a visual representation of the history, culture, and beliefs of a family or clan.

Totem poles serve many purposes. Some are built as part of a house, supporting the structure, while others stand near or in front of a home. Memorial poles are carved to honor family members who have passed away.

Carvings in a totem pole can include people, insects, mythological creatures, and animals. The animals most often carved are the beaver, bear, eagle, raven, thunderbird, wolf, killer whale, shark, and frog. Each figure on the pole represents part of a story.

Carvers use a specific style and process and hold an important place in the community. Many develop their craft at a young age. It can take from 3 to 9 months to complete a totem pole.

ALERT BAY

TALLEST TOTEM POLES

The largest totem pole in Canada can be found at Alert Bay, British Columbia. It stands 173 feet high and is composed of two sections. In the United States, McKinleyville, California, is home to a 160-foot-high totem pole carved from a single redwood tree.

SACRED FEATHERS

The tradition of creating and wearing feather headdresses started in the Great Plains region in the late 1800s. Only the most important men of the Sioux, Blackfeet, and Cheyenne tribes had the honor of wearing one.

Feathers for a headdress had to be earned through acts of courage. The most commonly used feathers came from crows, hawks, and eagles, with the highest prestige being associated with that of a golden eagle, one of the largest and fastest raptors in North America. Its feathers represented honesty, truth, strength, and wisdom. After several feathers of any kind were earned, the man's family members had the honor of making his headdress.

8 TIPS FOR WATCHING THE GEMINID METEOR SHOWER

METEOR SHOWERS ARE EVENTS IN WHICH METEORS FALL TOWARD EARTH FROM A RADIANT, OR CERTAIN POINT IN THE SKY. MOST METEOR SHOWERS ARE NAMED AFTER THE CONSTELLATIONS FROM WHICH THEY APPEAR TO COME.

OCCURRING EVERY DECEMBER, THE GEMINIDS ARE THE MOST ACTIVE METEOR SHOWER OF THE YEAR. AT MIDMONTH, THEIR PEAK, ONE-A-MINUTE FREQUENCY HAS CREATED RELIABLE SPARKLERS THROUGHOUT THE PAST CENTURY.

ASTRONOMY

HERE ARE SOME TIPS TO ENSURE HAVING A GREAT VIEWING EXPERIENCE:

1. The Geminids are out all night long. They are more frequent around 2:00 A.M., but you can watch them from early evening through dawn of the next day.

4. Normally, you should expect to see 50 to 60 shooting stars per hour in a dark sky free of moonlight. In an especially good year under perfect night sky conditions, you may see between 75 and 100!

2. You can see the Geminids from anywhere in the Northern Hemisphere.

SLOW SHOW

Geminids move more slowly than either the famous summer Perseids (in August) or the infrequent Leonids (in November) because they come at Earth sideways. At 22 miles per second, they scurry along at half the speed of the other major showers. Instead of sharp, brief zips across the sky, we see leisurely streakers.

3. Look toward the part of the sky that is darkest, away from the Moon. A full Moon will make it difficult or nearly impossible to see the meteors. They will appear anywhere in the full expanse of the night sky.

5. As for all meteor-watching and stargazing, try to get away from city lights to a place with an open stretch of sky. Bring a folding chair to be comfortable or perhaps a sleeping bag. And dress warmly–it's December, after all!

MYSTERY METEORS

The Geminids are the most mysterious meteors in the known universe. They come from the asteroid 3200 Phaethon in the constellation Gemini. All other showers are debris from comets. Strangely, Geminid meteors are twice as dense as most others yet not heavy enough to be metal-stone asteroid material.

6. Leave the telescope at home. For a show like the Geminids, there's no need for fancy equipment. Your eyes will do just fine. Our eyes need about 20 minutes to adapt to dark skies. The Geminid meteor shower tends to be a fast-paced display, with very bright white lights.

7. What's better than stargazing alone on a dark night? Bringing along a friend so that you can double your meteor-spotting capabilities! You can even make it into a competition.

METEOROID, METEOR, OR METEORITE?

• A **meteoroid** is a small piece of stony, metallic, or icy matter that hurtles through space.

• A **meteor** is a meteoroid that enters Earth's atmosphere and briefly streaks across the sky.

• A **meteorite** is a meteor that lands on the surface of Earth or another celestial body.

8. Be patient and keep your eyes glued to the sky!

Special Report

TOP SECRET

UFOS FACT or FICTION?

BETTY AND BARNEY HILL WERE DRIVING HOME FROM MONTREAL, CANADA, ON THE NIGHT OF SEPTEMBER 19, 1961, THROUGH THE WHITE MOUNTAINS OF NEW HAMPSHIRE WHEN THEY NOTICED A STRANGE LIGHT IN THE SKY.

NEXT 4 MILES

WHEN BETTY AND BARNEY RETURNED HOME,
THEY COULDN'T REMEMBER ROUGHLY 2 HOURS OF THE DRIVE.
IT HAD VANISHED FROM THEIR MEMORIES, BUT . . .

THEY NOTICED BOTH OF THEIR
WATCHES HAD STOPPED WORKING!

TAP
TAP
TAP

BARNEY'S SHOES
WERE SCUFFED!

BETTY'S DRESS
WAS TORN!

THE STRAP ON THEIR
BINOCULARS WAS BROKEN!

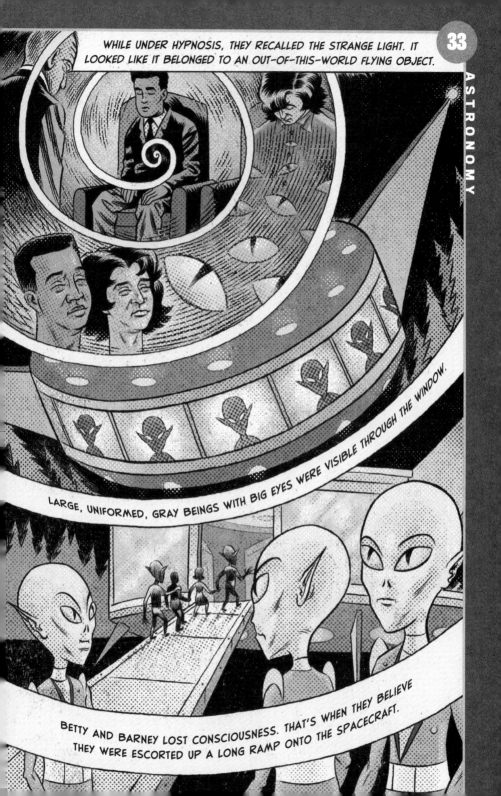

THEY WERE BROUGHT INTO EXAMINATION ROOMS WITH CURVED WALLS AND A LARGE LIGHT HANGING FROM THE CEILING.

THEY WERE HELPED TO LIE DOWN ON METAL TABLES. THE BEINGS THEN COLLECTED SAMPLES OF THEIR . . .

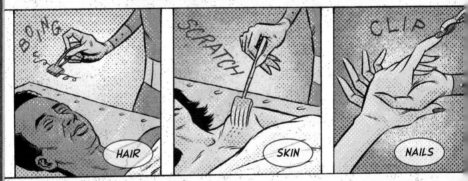

BOING

HAIR

SCRATCH

SKIN

CLIP

NAILS

THEIR HEADS, ARMS, LEGS, AND SPINES WERE PROBED WITH NEEDLES.

WHEN IT WAS OVER, THEY FOUND THEMSELVES BACK IN THEIR CAR ON THEIR WAY HOME, WITH THEIR MEMORIES OF THE ABDUCTION WIPED CLEAN.

AFTER SHARING THEIR STORY WITH THE PUBLIC, THEY GAINED WORLDWIDE FAME.

THIS INCIDENT IS THE FIRST FULLY DOCUMENTED CASE OF AN ALLEGED ALIEN ABDUCTION.

DOES OUTER SPACE END?

Have you ever wondered what it would be like to travel to outer space—and then keep going? What would you find? Scientists are able to explain a lot of what you'd see—but there are some things that they don't know yet, like whether space just goes on forever.

Right above you is the sky—or, as scientists would call it, the atmosphere. It extends about 20 miles above Earth.

THE ATMOSPHERE

Above the atmosphere is space. It's called that because it has far fewer molecules, with lots of empty space between them.

Floating around in the atmosphere is a mixture of molecules—tiny bits of air so small that you take in billions of them every time you breathe.

PLANETS, STARS, AND GALAXIES

At the beginning of your trip through space, you might recognize some of the sights. Earth is one in a group of planets that all orbit the Sun—along with some asteroids and comets mixed in, too.

You might know that the Sun is actually a star. It looks bigger and brighter than other stars only because it is closer. To get to the next nearest star, you would have to travel through trillions of miles of space.

If you could ride on the fastest space probe that NASA has ever made, you would still need thousands of years to get there.

Recently, astronomers have learned that many stars have their own orbiting planets. Some are even like Earth, so it's possible that they might be home to other beings also wondering what's out there.

If you were to think of stars as houses, then galaxies would be like cities full of houses. Scientists estimate that there are 100 billion stars in Earth's galaxy. If you could zoom out and view them from way beyond Earth's galaxy, these 100 billion stars would seem to blend together—just like the lights of a city do when seen from an airplane.

100,000,000,000

PACK YOUR BAGS!

You would have to travel through millions of trillions more miles of space just to reach another galaxy. Most of this space is almost completely empty, except for some stray molecules and tiny mysterious invisible particles that scientists call

"dark matter."

ANDROMEDA GALAXY

CYGNUS A GALAXY

NEEDLE GALAXY

SUNFLOWER GALAXY

FIREWORKS GALAXY

If you could watch for long enough, over millions of years, you might notice that new space is gradually being added between all of the galaxies. You can visualize this by imagining tiny dots on a deflated balloon and then thinking about blowing it up. The dots would keep moving farther apart, just like the galaxies are.

IS THERE AN END?

If you could travel through space as far as you wanted to go,
would you just keep passing by galaxies forever?
Are there infinite numbers of galaxies in every direction?
Or does outer space end?
If it does end, what does it end with?

END

Scientists don't have definite
answers to these questions yet.
Many think that it's likely that you
would just keep passing galaxies
in every direction forever.

In that case, the universe would
be infinite, with no end.

Others think that it's possible that the universe might eventually wrap back around on itself—so if you kept going away from Earth, eventually you would come back to where you started.

One way to think about this is to picture a globe and imagine that you are a creature that can move only on the surface.

If you started walking in any direction—east, for example—and just kept going, eventually you would come back to where you began. If this happened in the universe, it would mean that it is not infinitely big—although it would still be bigger than you can imagine.

In either case, you could never get to the end of the universe or space. Scientists now consider it unlikely that the universe has an end—a region where the galaxies stop or where there is a barrier of some kind marking the end of space.

But nobody knows for sure.

The answer to this question will need to be figured out by a future scientist.

Maybe you?

ICE TIME

What do hockey rinks, freeze pops, and Queen Elsa's castle all have in common? You guessed it—ice! Read on to find out about how ice develops, the names of ice formations, and one *really* cool place to stay!

Convert to metric on p. 170

ICE BITS

When water is exposed to cold temperatures, 32°F (0°C) or below, it freezes into ice. As water freezes, it expands to become a solid that is less dense than its liquid state. Because ice has less density than water, it floats. Water makes up more than 70 percent of Earth's surface, and over 2 percent of Earth's water is contained in ice.

WHAT IS THAT?

Frost flowers, also known as ice flowers or rabbit ice, appear as delicate ribbons of white ice crystals growing from the base and stems of plants in late fall or early winter. Abundant soil moisture, freezing weather, and not-yet-frozen ground are needed for frost flowers to form.

NATURE'S FROZEN WONDERS

GLACIERS are large, slowly moving masses of ice originally formed by the compression and freezing of snow, rock, sediment, and water on land over hundreds to thousands of years.

ICEBERGS are large pieces of frozen fresh water that break off from a glacier or ice sheet and float in open water. To be classified as an iceberg, a chunk must rise to at least 16 feet above sea level, have a thickness of 98 to 164 feet, and cover an area of at least 5,382 square feet. Only about 10 percent of an iceberg is visible above the water.

Large areas of glacial ice—roughly 20,000 square miles—are known as **ICE SHEETS.** The Antarctic Ice Sheet at the South Pole is the largest on Earth, covering almost 5.4 million square miles (about the size of the United States and Mexico combined). The Greenland Ice Sheet near the North Pole is about three times the size of Texas and covers more than 80 percent of Greenland's surface.

ICE HISTORY

On April 12, 1912, the RMS *Titanic*, a British passenger liner on its way to New York City on its first voyage, struck an **ICEBERG** and sank. The disaster led to the formation of the International Ice Patrol, a U.S. Coast Guard agency that monitors iceberg locations in the North Atlantic Ocean.

SEA ICE is frozen ocean water. It covers about 9.7 million square miles of Earth, or an area about two-and-a-half times the size of Canada. Most sea ice is contained within the Arctic and Antarctic regions at the North and South Poles.

ICE HISTORY

In March 1848, Niagara Falls stopped flowing. An **ICE JAM** made up of millions of tons of ice blocked the source of the Niagara River, and for 30 hours water stopped running over the famous falls that span the U.S.-Canada border.

An **ICE JAM** is made up of floating pieces of ice that block the natural flow of a river or stream. These occur from late winter to early spring when water repeatedly freezes and melts.

A **BRINICLE** is a hollow tube of ice that grows downward below floating sea ice. These form when a seawater solution called brine is released from pockets in the sea ice. The extremely salty and very cold brine will freeze any water with which it comes into contact, forming a fragile, icy tube.

MORE FROZEN WONDERS

NEEDLE ICE forms when water pushes up through soil to the surface into below-freezing temperatures. The water begins to freeze at soil level and then continues to freeze and grow taller above it.

HAIR ICE appears when water squeezes out of rotting wood and hits freezing air. The frozen water looks like cotton candy. Fungus on the surface of the rotting wood provides a foundation for the ice formation.

ICICLES form when the outside temperature is below freezing but the warmth of the Sun causes snow or ice to melt. When water drips off a surface such as a roof and meets the freezing air, it freezes again. The tip of an icicle forms faster than the base (top), resulting in its distinctive shape.

BLACK ICE is a clear glaze that forms on roads, sidewalks, and driveways. It develops at night or early in the morning when rain, snow, or moisture from the air freezes rapidly.

ICE HISTORY

Before refrigerators were invented, ice blocks were harvested from frozen ponds and stored in ice houses, which were insulated with hay or straw and sawdust. These blocks were sold to families to help keep their food chilled in an insulated cupboard called an "ice box."

THIS IS NOT ICE!

Dry ice is the solid form of carbon dioxide, not water. With a temperature of -109°F, it can cause frostbite if touched. As dry ice melts, it returns directly to its gas form.

BUBBLE LAKE

During January and February, frozen bubbles containing methane gas appear just below the surface of Abraham Lake in Alberta, Canada. Released by decaying plants and tree limbs at the bottom of the lake, the gas gets trapped in ice when the temperature drops. As the cold weather continues, bubbles stack up below the frozen surface of the lake.

COOL RIDE!

In December 2013, the Canadian Tire Corporation built an ice truck to test its Eliminator battery in the cold. More than 11,000 pounds of ice were used to make the body, windows, seats, and dashboard of the truck, while the rest of it consisted of mechanical automobile parts. The battery worked, and the truck traveled at an average speed of 12 miles per hour for 1 mile.

A COOL PLACE TO STAY

North America's only ice hotel is located in Quebec City, Canada. Open from early January through March, the Hôtel de Glace features more than 20 uniquely sculpted rooms. Hotel guests sleep in arctic sleeping bags and must bring specialized winter clothing for an overnight stay in temperatures that can get down to around 23°F!

MAKE AN ICE SUNCATCHER

YOU WILL NEED:
a cake pan or other round container
water
food coloring
small plastic cup filled with anything (coins, rocks, etc.) to weigh it down
ribbon or yarn

1. Add about 1 inch of water to the pan.

2. Place the weighted cup on one side of the pan (being careful not to let it be touching the side) and then put the pan into the freezer.

3. Freeze for 1 hour, or until the ice is partially frozen.

4. Remove the pan from the freezer, then quickly add drops of food coloring to it. Put the pan back into the freezer for a few hours or overnight.

5. Remove the pan from the freezer again. Allow the ice to thaw enough to loosen from the pan, then remove the cup.

6. Remove the ice suncatcher from the pan and loop the ribbon or yarn through the hole left by the cup. Hang on a tree branch or outside a window.

Penguin Puzzler

Find five differences between the two scenes below.

(SOLUTION ON PAGE 171.)

Convert to metric on p. 170

The WAYS of the WIND

Have you ever wondered why and how wind blows? To start with, we need to examine air. If air didn't weigh anything, we wouldn't have wind. But air has weight, and cold air weighs more than warm air. More weight means more pressure, which means that cold air has more pressure. When the Sun warms the air, the air expands, becomes lighter, and rises. Colder, heavier air below moves into the space that the warmer, rising air has vacated. This movement of air causes wind. The speed of the wind is determined by how close the cold air and warm air masses are to each other and their pressure or temperature difference. The bigger the difference, the faster the wind blows.

EVERY WIND HAS ITS WEATHER.

–Sir Francis Bacon, English philosopher (1561–1626)

THE JET STREAM

Weather forecasters on TV and the Internet often talk about the **JET STREAM**, using dramatic sweeping motions to indicate how it is swooping down out of Canada across the Great Plains. But are jets involved? No. The jet stream is the west-to-east flow of winds in the upper atmosphere, usually more than 30,000 feet above the ground. Their speeds are usually about 80 to 140 miles per hour but can reach to more than 275 miles per hour. Weather forecasters talk about them a lot because their speed and flow steer storms around the world. The jet stream may contain "jet streaks," which are even faster winds. These also affect the weather patterns at ground level.

Special Winds for Special Areas

People in the Pacific Northwest pay attention when forecasters mention the **PINEAPPLE EXPRESS,** a strong southwesterly wind off the Pacific Ocean. This wind can bring heavy rain and flooding to the area during winter.

In southern California, the winds to fear are the **SANTA ANA** winds, gusty northeast or east winds that occur during the fall and winter months. Santa Ana winds are often hot and very dry, presenting a danger of forest or brush fires.

In a small area along the western coast of Cape Breton Island, Nova Scotia, springtime means being ready for the **SUÊTE,** a windstorm with speeds of up to 150 miles per hour. This occurs when a southeast wind

TRUCK OVERTURNED FROM THE SUÊTE

flows up over mountains on one side before increasing speed as it blows down to the Gulf of St. Lawrence on the other. The wind force builds up to as much as three times its initial speed, and people, window shutters, and sometimes even vehicles get blown about! People in the area are used to it. Farmers have built their barns close to or attached to their houses to avoid heading into the wind when it's time to feed or milk the animals.

A WONDER DOWN UNDER

And the award for the most consistent wind in the world goes to ... the "**FREMANTLE DOCTOR**"! This cooling sea breeze on the west coast of Australia, near Perth, occurs between noon and 3:00 P.M. on almost every summer day.

Wind Wanted

Many sports and recreational activities require wind, including **KITEBOARDING**, windsurfing, sailing, paragliding, and hot air ballooning.

MEASURE THE WIND

An anemometer is an instrument that measures wind speed.

The simplest anemometer is a **WIND SOCK**, a tube of cloth attached to a metal ring that rotates at the top of a pole. Because a wind sock pivots so that its larger opening faces the wind, it indicates wind direction as well as speed.

A **CUP ANEMOMETER** is usually made of several small cups on arms attached to a vertical pole. The wind causes the cups and pole to turn. This calculates wind speed more accurately than a wind sock, which shows relative wind speed only by how inflated it is.

Top Four Windiest Places in the U.S.

Mount Washington,
  New Hampshire
Dodge City, Kansas
Amarillo, Texas
Cheyenne, Wyoming
  —*National Oceanic and
  Atmospheric Administration*

WOW! THAT'S WINDY!

The highest wind speed in the world was recorded on April 10, 1996, at Barrow Island, Australia. **TROPICAL CYCLONE OLIVIA** produced five extreme 3-second wind gusts, the peak of which was 253 miles per hour.

Top Four Windiest Places in Canada

St. John's, Newfoundland
Hamilton, Ontario
Regina, Saskatchewan
Winnipeg, Manitoba
  —*Environment Canada*

WINDY WEATHER WATCHING

*No weather is ill,
If the wind be still.*

*When wind comes before rain,
Soon you may make sail again.*

The wind in the west suits everyone best.

*A fog and a small Moon
Bring an easterly wind soon.*

A pale green sky means the wind is high.

HOW TO MEASURE WIND SPEED

The **BEAUFORT WIND FORCE SCALE** is a common way
of estimating wind speed. It was developed in 1805 by Admiral Sir
Francis Beaufort of the British Navy to measure wind at sea.
We can also use it to measure wind on land.
Admiral Beaufort arranged the numbers 0 to 12 to indicate
the strength of the wind from calm, force 0, to hurricane, force 12.
Here's a scale adapted to land.

*"Used Mostly at Sea but of Help to All Who
Are Interested in the Weather"*

BEAUFORT FORCE	DESCRIPTION OF WIND	WHEN YOU SEE OR FEEL THIS EFFECT	WIND SPEED (mph)	(km/h)
0	CALM	Smoke goes straight up	< 1	< 2
1	LIGHT AIR	Wind direction is shown by smoke drift but not by wind vane	1–3	2–5
2	LIGHT BREEZE	Wind is felt on the face; leaves rustle; wind vanes move	4–7	6–11
3	GENTLE BREEZE	Leaves and small twigs move steadily; wind extends small flags straight out	8–12	12–19
4	MODERATE BREEZE	Wind raises dust and loose paper; small branches move	13–18	20–29
5	FRESH BREEZE	Small trees sway; waves form on lakes	19–24	30–39
6	STRONG BREEZE	Large branches move; wires whistle; umbrellas are difficult to use	25–31	40–50
7	NEAR GALE	Whole trees are in motion; walking against the wind is difficult	32–38	51–61
8	GALE	Twigs break from trees; walking against the wind is very difficult	39–46	62–74
9	STRONG GALE	Buildings suffer minimal damage; roof shingles are removed	47–54	75–87
10	STORM	Trees are uprooted	55–63	88–101
11	VIOLENT STORM	Widespread damage	64–72	102–116
12	HURRICANE	Widespread destruction	73+	117+

Chiming In With the Wind

You can make music with "wind" (such as by playing a recorder, flute, or other wind instrument), but it's also fun to let wind make music *by itself.* Wind chimes are a great way to do this. They come in many sizes and shapes, and the sounds that yours make will depend on what you use. Experiment with a variety of materials or use several at once. Try beads, bamboo or other wood, jingle bells, metal spoons and forks or other kitchen utensils, metal washers, old keys, plastic balls, seashells, metal cans (clean), and/or buttons of different sizes.

YOU WILL NEED:

decorating materials (paint, glitter, ribbon, markers)
a drill or other tool to make a hole in the chimes for the string
glue (optional)
string, yarn, or fishing line
a hanger, such as a coat hanger, wooden dowel, or stick
scissors
three or more "chimes" (the heavier the chime, the stronger the wind needed to move it)

1. Gather materials.

2. Decorate your chimes, if desired.

3. If necessary, drill a hanging hole in each of your chimes. (Ask an adult for help.)

4. Tie or glue a piece of string to each chime. Experiment with using different lengths of string. Make sure that the chimes will touch when they are moved by the wind.

5. Arrange the chimes by tying them to the hanger. Heavier objects should be in the center, for balance. Attach them loosely until you are sure that the arrangement balances and sounds good. Rearrange as needed.

6. Find a breezy place to hang your creation, such as under a tree limb or porch ceiling.

Chimes Through the Times
• Wind chimes can also be called "aeolian chimes." Aeolus was the keeper of the winds in Greek mythology.
• In Japan, wind chimes are hung in the corners of Buddhist temples, where they are said to keep away troublesome spirits.

BUTTON CHIME

KEY CHIME

BEAD AND PLANT POT CHIME

METAL CAN CHIME

BENEFICIAL BUGS

NOT ALL BUGS ARE *BAD* FOR THE GARDEN . . .

IN THE GARDEN

WHAT ARE BENEFICIAL INSECTS?

The average backyard is home to thousands of insects, and you may be surprised to learn that only about a tenth of these are pests. Most are either beneficial or harmless. Beneficial insects fall into three main categories . . .

■ **POLLINATORS:** We depend on these insects—such as bees, butterflies, flies, and moths—to pollinate our garden's flowers.

■ **PREDATORS** eliminate pests by eating them. Ladybugs, praying mantises, and green lacewing larvae are predators.

■ **PARASITOIDS:** Like predators, parasitoids also prey upon other insects but in a slightly different way. They lay their eggs on or in the bad bugs, and when the eggs hatch, the larvae feed on the host insects, eventually killing them. Parasitic wasps are the main member of this category.

INTRODUCING THE BENEFICIAL BUGS

Everyone knows bees and butterflies, but what about the many other beneficial bugs? It's likely that you've already seen them in the garden but haven't been formally introduced. Here are a few with whom you might want to become acquainted:

HOVERFLIES

Good insects to have in your garden, hoverflies look like tiny yellowjackets without a stinger. They feed on pollen and nectar and are important pollinators. Their larvae are hungry predators, eliminating aphids, caterpillars, beetles, and thrips by sucking their juice.

PRAYING MANTISES

A praying mantis will take care of any grasshoppers making trouble in your garden, as well as hunt many other insect pests, including crickets and many destructive beetles. Note, however, that praying mantises are ruthless and will turn to eating other beneficials, such as butterflies, bees, and hummingbirds (yes, hummingbirds!)–and even each other.

SPIDERS

Spiders—although technically arachnids, not insects—are often overlooked as being beneficial in the garden, but they are effective pest controllers because they are attracted to insects that move. Jumping spiders and wolf spiders are especially good at catching pests.

WOLF SPIDER

LADYBUGS

Despite their delightful name and appearance, ladybugs are ferocious predators! Before they turn bright red, they start life as larvae that feast on aphids. Did you know that a ladybug larva can eat up to 40 aphids an hour?

ROBBER FLIES

With their extra-long legs, robber flies are bug-eating machines that go after a number of common garden pests. Their hairy bodies may look intimidating, but they do not attack humans (although they are capable of biting you if you try to catch one). Do not shoo this fly!

GROUND BEETLES

This large group of predatory beetles is beneficial as both adults and larvae. They will eat a wide range of pests, including nematodes, caterpillars, thrips, weevils, slugs, and silverfish.

SOLDIER BEETLES

Soldier beetles are important predators of Mexican bean beetles, Colorado potato beetles, caterpillars, and aphids. Adult soldier beetles are attracted to plants with yellow or orange flowers.

GREEN LACEWINGS

Adult green lacewings feed on pollen and nectar, but their larvae, which look like a cross between a slug and an alligator, prey upon soft-body garden pests such as caterpillars and aphids.

ASSASSIN BUGS

Assassin bugs look like a combination of a praying mantis and a squash bug. They use their sharp mouth parts to prey upon many different types of insect pests in the garden. Squash bugs resemble adult assassin bugs, which are good ones to have around.

PARASITIC WASPS

Parasitic wasps are tiny, so you will probably not see them at work. However, they are effective.

BRACHONID WASPS lay their eggs inside tomato hornworms and other caterpillars. The wasp larvae feed and develop inside a caterpillar before forming white cocoons on its back—which eventually turn into more wasps that continue to do good work in the tomato patch.

TRICHOGRAMMA WASPS lay their eggs inside the eggs of over 200 different insect pests.

TACHINID FLIES look like small houseflies but are parasitoids of corn borers, spongy moth caterpillars, grasshoppers, Japanese beetles, Mexican bean beetles, squash bugs, and green stinkbugs. Most female tachinid flies lay their eggs on the backs of host insects. When the eggs hatch, the larvae burrow down into the host and start feeding on it.

BRACHONID WASP COCOONS

TRICHOGRAMMA WASP

TACHINID FLY

INVITE BENEFICIAL INSECTS

Like all living creatures, beneficial insects need water, food, and shelter. By providing these things, your garden will become an inviting home for them.

An assortment of plants will attract a wide range of insects. Many beneficials appear in the garden before the pests do and thus need alternative food sources such as pollen and nectar if they are going to stick around.

They are especially attracted to many flowering herbs and wildflowers, such as yarrow, goldenrod, and Queen Anne's lace.

Nonflying beetles and spiders need a place to hide in the garden. Ground covers and mulches provide shelter.

YARROW

GOLDENROD

BUGS ROCK!

Decorate your backyard, balcony, garden, or patio with some painted bug rocks.

YOU WILL NEED:
smooth rocks
acrylic paints
paper plate
paintbrush
small cup of water (to clean brush)
clear spray sealer (optional)

1. Wash or wipe clean the rocks.

2. Squirt the paints that you will use onto the paper plate.

3. Paint pictures of bugs on the rocks or paint the rocks to look like bugs.

4. Let each color of paint dry completely before adding another.

5. Spray the finished rock with clear spray sealer (if using).

Follow the Rainbow of Vegetables

Cucumbers are green,
Tomatoes are red,
Potatoes are brown,
Or so it's said?
Not always!

Some of our most **common vegetables** come in **many colors.** In fact, the **most colorful** vegetables are the **most healthful** for you because they have the **most vitamins,** minerals, fiber, and **antioxidants.** Every color delivers a **different nutrient,** and if you eat a variety of **colorful veggies,** your body will get **almost everything** that it needs.

Black/Purple Tomatoes

Move over, red tomatoes! Make room for **'Black Beauty'**, which is an almost-black tomato with flavorful, dark red flesh on the inside. Black or purple tomatoes have the same healthy antioxidant that blueberries and blackberries have. The sweet and juicy 'Black Cherry' tomato looks like a black cherry on the vine. These small round tomatoes grow in big clusters.

One more thing: Many black tomatoes originated on the Black Sea's Crimean peninsula in southeastern Europe, where they've been grown and eaten for more than 100 years.

Orange Cauliflower

When is an orange not an orange? When it's a cauliflower! Orange cauliflower, which was discovered in Canada in 1970, resembles white cauliflower in shape, but its color—from yellowish to bright orange—spectacularly does not. Its florets, which get their orange color from a pigment called beta carotene, hold about 25 percent more vitamin A than those of white cauliflower.

One more thing: The name "cauliflower" comes from the Latin words *caulis*, meaning cabbage, and *flos*, meaning flower.

Yellow Cucumber

Let us introduce you to the unusual lemon cucumber, which looks like a lemon and is about the size of a tennis ball. It is sweet and crispy, with a thin skin. You can eat it fresh or pickle it for a tasty treat. Lemon cucumbers are popular in India and often used in soups and chutney.

One more thing: Cucumbers are related to melons and are 96 percent water.

Blue/Purple Potatoes

Feeling blue? Have a potato! Blue and purple varieties of potatoes are rich in fiber and protein and full of healthy antioxidants. The 'Adirondack Blue' potato has purple skin and purplish-blue flesh. It has a rich, nutty flavor and keeps its color when cooked. **'All Blue'** is often used to make purple potato chips.

One more thing: Potatoes have more potassium than bananas.

Brown Peppers

Are those chocolate peppers? Keep dreaming. These peppers start off as green but when mature turn completely brown. The '7 Pot Brown' variety is a spicy hot pepper that gets its name from being able to spice seven pots of stew with just one pod. 'Brown Holland' bell peppers are sweet and juicy. This variety is also known as the **'Chocolate Beauty'** pepper.

One more thing: Peppers were first grown in the tropics. Portuguese and Spanish explorers brought them to other parts of the world.

Red Carrots

Seeing red? That's a carrot! Red carrots get their color from lycopene, which also adds color to tomatoes and other red fruit and vegetables. Red carrots are pinkish to orange on the inside and sweeter than orange carrots. Varieties of red carrots include **'Atomic Red'** and 'Red Samurai'.

One more thing: Carrot seeds are tiny. About 2,000 seeds can fit in a teaspoon!

Cool Hues

Check out these colorful veggies

CHIOGGIA BEETS

The Chioggia is a sweet heirloom beet first grown in the town of Chioggia, Italy, in the early 1800s. It is also called the "candy stripe" or "bull's-eye" beet. The eye-catching rings of red and white inside the beet make it a favorite in salads and as a side dish.

GLASS GEM CORN

This very special heirloom corn was created by Carl Barnes, a part-Cherokee Oklahoma farmer, who carefully saved seeds from many colorful corn varieties over many years and then replanted the brightest. This process enhanced the colors so that today all of the kernels on each cob glisten like beautiful jewels.

CANDY CANE RED PEPPERS

This sweet pepper starts out as green with cream-color stripes before turning completely red. As it ripens and the stripes fade, the pepper takes on a sweeter flavor. Its leaves will mesmerize you with their pretty cream and green stripes.

& Curlicues
that also have delightful designs!

DRAGON TONGUE BEANS

This heirloom bush bean originated in the Netherlands. Its 6- to 8-inch-long pods are yellow with purple streaks; however, when cooked, the purple fades away. The bean is tender and delicious and can be eaten fresh or dried for later cooking.

MEXICAN SOUR GHERKINS

Also called "cucamelons" and "mouse melons," these members of the same plant family as cucumbers, squash, and pumpkins look like miniature watermelons and taste tangy and mildly citrus-y. They have been grown and used for centuries by the Aztecs and other indigenous peoples.

'BRIGHT LIGHTS' SWISS CHARD

A member of the beet family, Swiss chard is best known for its bright and vibrant stems, which come in many colors. 'Bright Lights' is especially dazzling and as pretty as it is tasty. Originally from New Zealand, this chard is sweeter and milder than other types.

Beauty or Beast?

The fly makes a landing. The fleshy fangs on the leaf tremble and then clamp down with lightning speed! The Venus flytrap strikes again—and another unsuspecting victim has met its doom.

PITCHER PLANT

Probably the most well known of nature's flesh-eating plants, the Venus flytrap is one of more than 600 kinds of plants that capture, kill, and eat other living things. Most of these carnivorous plants live in swamps and bogs. Some, like the pitcher plants of Borneo, are so big that frogs and rodents have reportedly disappeared into their deadly clutches!

The Venus flytrap is not that big. Most of its leaves are about the size of a human finger—perfect for catching bugs such as flies, spiders, and crickets. It attracts its prey with sweet nectar. The insects smell something appetizing and expect to have lunch—they don't expect to *be* lunch! The plant's leaves are lined with trigger hairs that act as motion detectors. If an insect touches these hairs enough, it needs to watch out—the leaf snaps shut on it as quickly as you can say "lunchtime"!

Once the two halves of the leaf clamp shut, they squeeze tighter and tighter as the insect struggles, until they become flat. Cilia, the little hairs that line the edge of each leaf, interlock and lace together so that the insect and the plant's digestive juices can't escape and bacteria and mold can't get inside while the prey is being digested.

Get **Growing**

Although Venus flytrap populations are dwindling in the wild due in part to overharvesting and habitat loss, you can still enjoy watching one at home by asking someone who has one to give you a cutting from which you can grow your own.

YOU WILL NEED:

a big jar with a lid
coarse sand

green sphagnum moss
flytrap leaf cutting
water

1. Put the sand in the jar and then add the moss.

2. Stick the Venus flytrap leaf stalk in the moss, letting the leaf lie on top.

3. Add enough water to moisten the moss, poke some holes in the lid (ask an adult for help), and put the lid on the jar.

Little plants will grow from the leaf. Put your jar in a sunny window for a few hours each day. Keep the moss damp but not soaking wet. When leaves fully form, take off the lid occasionally and watch what happens when insects fly by!

The leaf remains closed until it has finished its meal, which usually takes from 5 to 12 days. It "swallows" by reabsorbing its juices and the liquefied nutrients from the prey. The leaf slowly reopens, and any remaining bits of the bug are blown away or washed off by rain.

After four to six meals, Venus flytrap leaves lose their ability to catch anything. They stay open and act like regular leaves, while the plant produces new trapping leaves.

SEE THE BEES

CAN YOU FIND 10 IN THE GARDEN?

(SOLUTION ON PAGE 171.)

WHAT FLOWER ARE YOU?

Take this quiz to find out which flower matches your personality!

1. A FRIEND WOULD DESCRIBE YOU AS:

A. Energetic, determined, confident

B. Social, helpful, cheerful

C. Trustworthy, loyal, sincere

D. Creative, imaginative, caring

2. WHAT'S YOUR FAVORITE SEASON OF THE YEAR?

A. Spring

B. Summer

C. Fall

D. Winter

3. AT A PARTY, YOU WOULD BE FOUND:

A. At the center of action, surrounded by lots of friends.

B. Talking to a few people and helping out.

C. Staying for a short time and wishing that you were home.

D. Mostly enjoying the food, music, and party vibe.

4. AS AN ADULT, YOU WOULD LIKE TO LIVE:

A. In a big city where the action is.

B. In a place where you know that you'll have friends and feel like you belong.

C. Somewhere that's not crowded, away from other people.

D. In a beautiful space surrounded by nature or art.

5. IF YOU HAD A FREE DAY AND COULD DO ANYTHING, YOU WOULD CHOOSE TO:

A. Go somewhere with all of your friends—to a party, park, or other fun place.

B. Ask one friend to get together and hang out.

C. Relax on the couch with a book or watch TV.

D. Do something creative like baking or drawing.

TULIPS

SUNFLOWERS

HYDRANGEAS

DAHLIAS

So, What Flower Are You?

- If you answered mostly **A: TULIP.** You are a passionate, energetic person with ambition.
- If you answered mostly **B: SUNFLOWER.** You put your friends and family first and always help when needed.
- If you answered mostly **C: HYDRANGEA.** You are a loyal, honest person whom others consider reliable.
- If you answered mostly **D: DAHLIA.** You are imaginative, artistic, and an independent spirit.
- If your answers end in a tie between two letters, then you may possess the qualities of both flowers!

DID YOU KNOW?

There are about 780 million pigs on Earth. Denmark has roughly twice as many pigs as people! China has the most domesticated pigs in the world, with the United States in second place.

This Little Piggy

ON THE FARM

Pigs are often misunderstood. Many folks consider them to be dirty, lazy, and not very smart, but this is not true. Pigs are clean, intelligent, and sensitive animals, as you'll see here.

Convert to metric on p. 170

WEE AND NOT SO WEE ONES

A litter of piglets, called a farrow, contains 8 to 12 piglets. When a piglet is born, it weighs from 2.5 to 3.5 pounds. It usually doubles its weight in just 1 week. Fully grown pigs can weigh between 300 and 700 pounds—and sometimes more. The largest pig on record, named Big Bill, weighed 2,552 pounds! Adult pigs range in length from about 2 to 7 feet long. Big Bill was 9 feet long. The smallest species of pig in the world is India's endangered pygmy hog, which measures between 20 and 28 inches long.

PIG PARTICULARS

Pigs are also called *hogs* or *swine*.

Male pigs are called *boars*.

Female pigs are called *gilts*.

Female pigs that have given birth are called *sows*.

Baby pigs are called *piglets*.

Piglets that have been weaned are called *shoats*.

JOY

HERE, PIGGY, PIGGY!

Pigs have excellent memories and can learn tricks. Many learn their name and will come when called. Joy, a pig from Iowa, holds the Guinness World Record for most tricks by a pig in 1 minute. She performed 13 different ones, including dancing, rolling a ball, and playing a toy piano.

TUSKS VS. TEETH

Wild pigs are also called wild boars. They dig with their sharp tusks, as well as use them as weapons for defending themselves. Pigs on a farm don't have tusks, but they do have tusklike teeth that they use to eat grains and food scraps.

OMELET

PRIZED PIGS

A study at Penn State University placed four young pigs (Hamlet, Omelet, Ebony, and Ivory) in front of a computer screen with a joystick and a treat dispenser. A number of blue walls appeared on the screen, and the pigs had to figure out how to move a dot onto one of the walls by using their snouts to move the joystick. When they were successful, they received a treat.

ABOUT THE SNOUT

Pigs have an excellent sense of smell. A pig's snout is about 2,000 times more sensitive than a human nose. The snout is an important tool for finding food in the ground. Truffles (a type of fungus, or mushroom, that can cost as much as $4,500 per pound) grow underground on tree roots. Pigs have been trained to sniff them out. First reported in print in the 15th century, truffle hunting with pigs is a tradition that began in Roman times.

BABY JANE

OLD BABY JANE

The oldest pig on record, Baby Jane from Illinois, was 23 years and 221 days old when she died in 2021.

This pig went to market,
That pig stayed home;
This pig had roast meat,
That pig had none;
This pig went to the barn's door,
And cried "week, week" for more.

–First published in *The Famous Tommy Thumb's Little Story-Book,* c. 1760 (the words had changed to "This little piggy . . ." by the mid–20th century)

FAMOUS PIGS

MISS PIGGY
This feisty Muppet is Kermit the Frog's girlfriend.

PORKY PIG
A cute, mild-mannered cartoon character that first appeared in 1935, Porky is known for ending cartoons by saying, "Th-th-th-that's all, folks!"

HAMM
Hamm is a sarcastic plastic piggy bank from the *Toy Story* movies.

PEPPA PIG
Peppa is a sweet British cartoon character who lives with her little brother George, Mummy Pig, and Daddy Pig.

PIGLET
Winnie the Pooh's friend Piglet is a terribly shy pig.

WILBUR
In the book *Charlotte's Web,* Wilbur and his friend Charlotte, a spider, live on a farm where Charlotte manages to save Wilbur's life by writing about him in her web.

GRUNTS IN OTHER LANDS

English: *oink-oink*
Albanian: *hunk-hunk* ("hoonk-hoonk")
Dutch: *knor-knor* ("k-NOHR-k-NOHR")
Finnish: *roh-roh* ("rrroh-rrroh")

French: *groin-groin* ("grenh-grenh")
German: *grunz-grunz* ("gruentz-gruentz")
Polish: *chrum-chrum* ("kroom-kroom")
Swedish: *noff-noff* ("nuff-nuff")

MORE TO DIG ABOUT PIGS

- Pigs don't sweat. To keep cool, they swim in water and roll around and sleep in mud. Mud also helps to keep their skin from getting sunburned.
- Pigs have two to three times as many taste buds as humans.
- An average pig eats about 5 to 7 pounds of food and drinks up to 8 gallons of water each day.
- Although pigs have poor eyesight, they have an excellent sense of direction and can find their way home across long distances.
- Pigs can run at up to 11 miles per hour.
- Pigs are very social. They form close relationships with other pigs and humans. They like to play, get their bellies rubbed, and sleep close together. Ever heard of a "pig pile"?
- Pigs have more than 20 different grunts and squeals, which can mean everything from asking for food to calling to their friends. A sow often "sings" or speaks softly to her piglets.

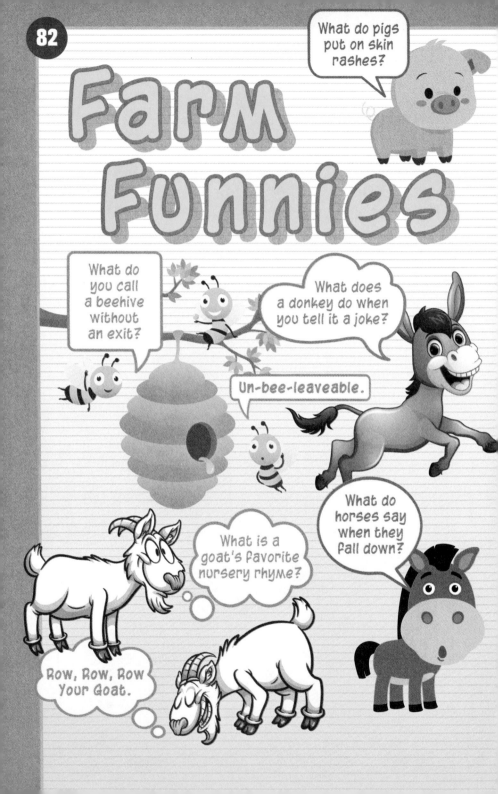

Hay! Is That

Q: DOES HAY CAUSE HAY FEVER?

A: No. Hay fever is the body's defensive allergic response to various kinds of plant pollen and mold spores. It is not a fever and has nothing to do with hay.

Straw?

Hay and straw are two different things but very often confused with each other. Both are crops grown and used on farms across the United States and Canada, but once hay and straw are harvested, their similarities end.

It's Hay

Hay crops, which include legumes like alfalfa and clover, dried grasses like timothy and ryegrass, or some combination of both, are farmed and harvested to feed livestock such as horses, cattle, sheep, and goats.

Hay must be cut at exactly the right time—when it contains many leaves with few seed heads or stems. The leaves contain high concentrations of starches, sugars, proteins, and minerals, all of which are important for an animal's diet.

Once cut, hay must be dried properly before storage. It is best to dry, or cure, hay in full sun, often right in the field where it was cut. After drying, hay is gathered into small rectangular or large round bales and stored away from moisture.

PUTTING HAY TO WORK

Hay is grown almost exclusively to feed animals. Although it is typically stored for winter feed, it sometimes is also used to supplement livestock diets in warmer months, especially during drought conditions.

It's Straw

Crops like wheat, rice, barley, and oats are harvested for their grain, which is found on their seed heads. The dry, yellowish stalks that remain are straw. This has no nutritional value but can serve many purposes around the farm or be sold for commercial or private use.

BARLEY

PUTTING STRAW TO WORK

Straw has many uses. In addition to serving as mulch for new lawns and strawberry plants and insulation for winter crops, it can also be found lining garden paths and walkways. Straw is also used as animal bedding and scarecrow stuffing and can be woven to make baskets and hats.

Straw bales are employed as fall decorations, walls to enclose compost bins, and building material. Some gardeners plant fruit, vegetables, and flowers in straw bales.

Straw-thatched roofs were common in Asia and Europe centuries ago. The method is still used in some parts of the world.

THAT'S NO HAYRIDE
Have you ever gone to a fair or farm and enjoyed a hayride? Guess what? You were likely sitting on straw, not hay.

Did You Know?

The pig who built his house out of straw in Walt Disney's *Three Little Pigs* was named Fifer. He loved to play the flute. The other two pigs were Fiddler and Practical.

Match Up

Connect each phrase with its meaning:

1. Hit the hay _____

2. Needle in a haystack _____

3. Hay is for horses _____

4. Make hay while the Sun shines _____

5. The last straw _____

6. Grasping at straws _____

A. A retort for when someone says, "Hey!"

B. Make good use of an opportunity while it lasts

C. Something very hard to find

D. Attempting to succeed when nothing is likely to work

E. Go to bed

F. Last in a series of bad things

ANSWERS: 1. E; 2. C; 3. A; 4. B; 5. F; 6. D

MONET PAINTINGS

Make Way for Hay

French painter Claude Monet created a series of paintings in 1890 and 1891 titled *Haystacks,* in which he depicted stacks that he had seen near his home in Giverny, France, in different seasons and at different times of day.

Vincent van Gogh also painted haystacks, most notably *Haystacks in Provence* in 1888.

TRADING UP

The legend of the Straw Millionaire is a Japanese folktale about a poor man whose life is changed by a piece of straw. The man goes to a temple and prays to Kannon, the goddess of mercy, for help. He is told to take care of the first thing that he touches upon leaving the temple and to go west. The first thing that the man touches is a piece of straw. He then catches a bothersome horsefly with the straw and ties them together, much to the amazement of a child. The child's mother gives the man three oranges for the straw. The man comes upon a woman who is thirsty and gives the oranges to her. In return, she gives him a piece of fine cloth. He trades the cloth for an ill horse and nurses it back to health. He is offered a house and rice field for the horse. Through acts of generosity and kindness, the single piece of straw was turned into a house and field, greatly improving his life.

COLOR BY NUMBER

If you're sharing this book, ask an adult
to make copies of this page.

(SOLUTION ON PAGE 171.)

ARCTIC FOX

SLY AS A FOX

What comes to mind when you think of a fox? Smart? Quick? Bushy-tailed? Foxes can be those and so much more!

WHAT IS A FOX?

Arctic fox	Cape fox	Kit fox	Rüppell's fox
Bengal fox	Corsac fox	Pale fox	Swift fox
Blanford's fox	Fennec fox	Red fox	Tibetan sand fox

The 12 "true" fox species, listed above, are all closely related. They are part of a larger, more loosely related group that includes wolves, coyotes, domestic dogs, and others. There are also about 25 animals called "foxes"—such as the bat-eared fox, crab-eating fox, and gray fox—that do not share all of the same traits as "true" foxes.

UNFORGETTABLE FOXES

ARCTIC FOX

This true fox lives mainly on the Arctic tundra. Its 2- to 3-inch-long ears—shorter than those of any other fox—reduce heat loss during the winter, helping it to stay warm. Its white winter coat turns brown after the snow disappears, which allows the animal to blend in with its surroundings during the summer.

Convert to metric on p. 170

BAT-EARED FOX

Named for its large, 5-inch-long ears, this fox lives in arid and semi-arid regions of eastern and southern Africa. A bat-eared fox's diet consists mainly of dung beetles and termites: One fox can eat about 1.15 million termites each year! It has 46 to 50 teeth—the most of any fox—which are designed for crushing the hard shells of insects.

CRAB-EATING FOX

This animal lives in parts of South America. During the wet season, it hunts crabs and other crustaceans in the mud along the shores of rivers, but it also will prey on insects, fish, rodents, rabbits, birds, reptiles, fruit, and whatever else it can find.

FENNEC FOX

The smallest of all foxes (about 24 inches, nose to tail tip), this true fox lives in the deserts and semi-deserts of northern Africa and the Sinai and Arabian peninsulas. Its large, 4- to 6-inch-long ears help it to capture sounds and to shed heat from its body.

GRAY FOX

Common in parts of North and Central America and often confused with the red fox, this animal has semi-retractable claws that allow it to climb trees—hence its nickname, "tree fox." Certain other foxes, including the red fox, can climb, too, but not as well as the gray fox.

KIT FOX

The smallest wild fox in North America (about 28 inches, nose to tail tip), this true fox lives in the arid and semiarid regions of the United States and parts of Mexico. Its 3- to 4-inch-long ears help it to hear and to remove heat from its body. The fur around its paw pads and toes protects it from hot sand and aids in traction.

The Remarkable Red Fox

Perhaps the most familiar fox is the red fox—and for good reason! It can be found in more places than any other nonhuman land mammal.

The red fox lives in many habitats, including forests, grasslands, mountains, and deserts, as well as in rural and urban environments. Although it often sleeps during the day in the open or in a partly sheltered area, it moves into a den to raise its young (called "pups," "kits," or "cubs"). The den may be in a self-dug or abandoned ground burrow, a hollow log or rock crevice, or even a crawl space under the deck of a house or other building.

RED Fox TRAITS

The red fox commonly has a white underbelly, some white on the ears and cheeks, and a white-tip tail. Its black paw color extends partway up its legs. Its usually yellow or green eyes have vertical pupils, which help it to see in dim light; these are unlike the round pupils of some fox relatives, such as wolves and domestic dogs.

What **DOES** the **FOX** Say?

Red foxes may communicate through more than 20 calls, including yips, barks, growls, and screeches. They can also leave messages through scents and use body language such as tail-wagging to express themselves.

Mealtime **"MOUSING"**

Red foxes eat mice and other small rodents, rabbits, eggs, fruit, seeds, birds, and reptiles. They may also dine on garbage and pet food. The animals usually hunt alone at dusk or night, storing any extra food in a secret spot in the ground or under grass or leaves.

Like all foxes, the red fox uses its excellent sense of smell, vision, and hearing when hunting. Its triangular ears help to capture sounds, and especially low-pitched noises. A red fox can accurately pounce headfirst into a pile of deep snow and catch an unseen mouse that it hears tunneling underneath. This technique is called "mousing."

CROSS FOX

Not Always a **"RED"** FOX

The largest of all foxes (about 42 inches, nose to tail tip), the red fox gets its name from its reddish-orange coat. However, a red fox may also appear in other colors. For example, a "silver fox" often is a red fox that has a black coat with silver-tip hairs; a "cross fox" is a red fox that has dark fur in the shape of a cross down its back and across its shoulders. There are also black or albino red foxes, as well as ones with other color combinations.

FAMILY Time

In the spring, a red fox female (called a "vixen") usually has a litter of five or six pups. The male fox (called a "dog fox") helps the vixen to take care of the pups by defending the family against predators, bringing food, and teaching survival skills. By fall or early winter, the pups are ready to go out on their own.

GRAY FOX

TAIL Tip

Gray foxes may be partly red and red foxes may be partly gray, sometimes making these species difficult to identify. However, a gray fox's tail has a black tip, while a red fox's usually has a white one.

RED FOX

FOX IN A BOX

Match each fictional fox with its description.

1. Fox in Sox _____
2. Foxy Loxy _____
3. Miles "Tails" Prower _____
4. Mr. Fox _____
5. Slylock Fox _____

A. In a book by Roald Dahl, this fantastic fox outwits farmers to save his starving family.

B. Twin-tailed friend of Sonic the Hedgehog

C. This crafty fox tries to catch his next meal: a chicken that believes the sky is falling.

D. A fox detective, with mouse sidekick, that solves puzzling mysteries

E. A fox with a tongue-twisting talent, as only Dr. Seuss could imagine

ANSWERS: 1. E; 2. C; 3. B; 4. A; 5. D

FAST **FOX** FACTS!

A red fox can **RUN** at a speed of up to 30 miles per hour for a short distance.

RED FOX

ARCTIC FOX

A fox **SHEDS** its winter coat to grow a shorter one for summer.

A **GROUP OF FOXES** is called a skulk, leash, earth, troop, or lead.

CAPE FOX

A **FOXTAIL** is called a "brush"; the tip, a "tag." Foxes use their tails to communicate, keep themselves warm in cold climates, and help with balance.

RED FOX

When **MOUSING,** red foxes tend to pounce in a northeasterly direction, suggesting that they may be using Earth's magnetic field to hunt.

SWIFT FOX

THE GREAT NIGHT FLIGHT

GROSBEAK

WHILE YOU SLEEP, THERE'S AN AMAZING SONGBIRD MIGRATION HAPPENING IN THE SKY!

WARBLER

ORIOLE

VIREO

MAGICAL MIGRATIONS

How far would you travel for a tasty snack? For many songbirds, the answer is hundreds of miles—perhaps over a thousand! Every fall, as freezing temperatures bring an end to bug season in the north, songbirds head south to gorge on insects, seeds, and fruit. When northern areas burst into life in spring, the birds return. They build nests and raise chicks, and they have no trouble finding plenty of food to fill the bellies of their hungry babies. This seasonal movement is called "migration." Some birds—like geese, hawks, and swallows—migrate during the day, but many songbirds fly at night.

BYE, BYE, BIRDIES!

If you live in northern parts of the world, you know that the arrival of autumn brings all sorts of wonderful things: colorful foliage, crunchy leaf piles, and warm apple cider. Autumn is also the season when some of the most beautiful birds in your backyard disappear. Many of the missing birds are songbirds—species known for singing marvelous melodies. These include colorful warblers, orioles, grosbeaks, vireos, and tanagers, as well as earth-tone birds like some thrushes, flycatchers, and sparrows. It's sad to see them go, but they leave for a good reason—and they'll be back!

TANAGER

DIFFERENT DESTINATIONS

Not all birds travel to the same place or take the same route. Some, like the red-eyed vireo, make exhaustingly long trips, venturing deep into South America. Others don't go as far. Lots of ovenbirds spend the winter in Florida—like many humans from the cold parts of North America. But there's one special songbird that should win a trophy for "Most Remarkable Migration"—the tiny blackpoll warbler. During its autumn migration, this long-distance flyer makes its way from the far northern forests of North America to the East Coast of the United States, where it stops to eat and fatten up. Then it launches itself over the Atlantic Ocean. High above the roaring waves, it flaps nonstop to South America, a journey that can take 3 days. That's an astonishing feat for a bird that could fit in your hand.

BLACKPOLL WARBLER

HOW TO ENJOY SONGBIRD MIGRATIONS

• Listen up! At night, many migrating birds make soft, short chirps called "nocturnal flight calls." Scientists use recording devices to catch these sounds and then figure out how many of what types of birds are passing by on any given evening.

• If the Moon is full, or nearly so, look at it through binoculars and you may see the dark silhouettes of songbirds passing in front of it.

• If you miss the birds at night, try searching at local parks during daytime. Look for birds foraging for food and preparing for another long night. Start a list of all of the species that you find. You will be amazed by how many you can see!

SCISSOR-TAILED FLYCATCHER

THE BRIGHT SIDE OF NIGHT

It seems odd to travel in the dark when the temperatures are cold and it's hard to see ahead of you. But the night has its advantages. Hungry predators such as hawks hunt only during daytime hours. Also, the cold night air keeps birds from overheating as they flap furiously for hours on end. But there's another reason that songbirds fly at night, and it's pretty amazing: The starry sky is full of important information that helps them to find their way! Songbirds use the stars to help them to navigate.

Migrating birds may cover hundreds of miles in a single night. As dawn approaches, they have to make a choice. If flying over water, they either keep going or turn around to go back to land. If there is dry land below, they descend from the sky and find a place to spend the day. They rest, but mostly they eat . . . and eat . . . and eat—because they need to top up their fuel reserves to be ready for the next night's flight.

LIGHTS OFF!

Migration is amazing, but it's also dangerous. Storms can blow birds off course or exhaust them. Plus, modern human life makes the birds' survival a challenge. Our bright artificial lights confuse their nighttime navigation systems, sending them crashing into buildings or flapping in circles until too tired to continue. This is why, during migration periods, we should all turn off the lights! Many urban areas— such as Chicago, Salt Lake City, and Toronto—have programs that encourage businesses to keep their lights off at night during key travel times for birds.

Here's something else that we can do: During the day, migratory birds often fly into windows and get hurt. They can't tell that glass is solid, as they see only reflected greenery or open air past the glass. You can help them to "see" windows by putting up window tape, hanging strings, or window film. Make sure that these visual barriers are no more than 2 inches apart and place them on the outside of your window. It's a fun craft project with a purpose. Your feathered friends will thank you, and you will keep enjoying their marvelous night migrations!

CREATURE CORNER

LITTLE-KNOWN CRITTERS FROM AIR, SEA, AND LAND!

ORIENTAL HORNET

Have you ever seen a solar panel on top of a house or school? Solar panels absorb sunlight and redirect the energy to batteries that make electricity. There is an insect that acts the same way—the oriental hornet. These brightly striped hornets live in southwest Asia and parts of Africa. They have a large yellow stripe across their abdomen full of tiny holes that absorb sunlight. The stripe contains chemicals that help to change the sunlight into energy. Why do the hornets need extra energy? It gives them a boost to do things like build nests. Scientists believe that oriental hornets may also be able to store the energy and use it to warm themselves when the temperature drops.

LEAF SHEEP

A sea slug that lives in the ocean off the coasts of the Philippines, Japan, Indonesia, Singapore, and Thailand is nicknamed the "leaf sheep." It gets this name from two features on its body. On top of its head, this tiny (only 0.4 inch long) creature has what look like ears similar in shape to those on sheep. These "ears," called rhinophores, have tips that move forward and sideways like antennae on insects. They help the leaf sheep to smell algae, its main food source–but when algae are scarce, the leaf sheep still has a technique to nourish itself.

A leaf sheep's back is covered in cerata, which are parts of its digestive system that look like leaves. These are bright green, but their tips can be white, pink, or purple. When a leaf sheep eats algae, it also consumes their chloroplasts (tiny structures inside the algae's cells that contain chlorophyll), which it can store in its cerata for up to 10 days. Because the leaf sheep lives between 30 and 60 feet below the surface of the water, where sunlight can still penetrate, it can absorb the Sun's energy. Its cerata are able to take chlorophyll in the chloroplasts and, with the help of the Sun, create food for the leaf sheep from it. The chloroplasts also contain chemicals that predators do not like, making the slugs inedible.

YELLOW-SPOTTED SALAMANDER

These amphibians live in swampy areas within woodlands in most of the eastern part of North America. They spend a lot of their time underneath logs and rocks and feed mostly on insects, grubs, and other small creatures in the soil. When it is time to lay their eggs, females travel to ponds that lack fish. (The fish would gobble up the tiny eggs and hatchlings!) But ponds without fish usually don't contain much oxygen, which is needed by the salamander babies. So, what do they do? They work together with the algae that grow in the ponds. While the baby salamanders are still forming in their eggs, they bond with the algae. The algae give oxygen and sugar to the baby salamander, and the developing salamander gives carbon dioxide and nitrogen, through its waste, to the algae.

After hatching, the salamanders stay in the water for about 4 months. Once they move to land, they protect themselves from predators such as chipmunks, raccoons, skunks, snakes, and turtles by releasing a sticky toxin from their backs and tails.

Seaside Sudoku

Fill in each blank with the letter of a picture at the top.
You may use a picture more than once, but make sure that no row
(across) or column (down) contains more than one of each.

A　　B　　C　　D　　E

1.____

2.____　　3.____

4.____　　5.____　　6.____

7.____　　8.____

9.____

Go Take a Hike—

Appalach

Known as the longest footpath in the world, the Appalachian Trail (AT) stretches over 2,190 miles through the Appalachian Mountains. The trail is full of ups and downs—one section in Virginia is known as the "Roller Coaster" because it has so many steep climbs and descents. Along the way, this rocky, root-filled, and often muddy trail crosses streams and passes through 14 states. At one end lies Georgia's 3,782-foot-high Springer Mountain; at the other is Maine's tallest mountain, 5,267-foot Mt. Katahdin.

Hikers need to take an average of about 5 million steps to get from one end to the other. Each year, several thousand hikers attempt this grand adventure—which typically takes about 5 to 7 months—but only about one in four makes it all the way. Some people do it all at once, while others attack it section by section, sometimes hiking 1 week every year until they're done. An estimated 1 million people each year hike some part of the AT.

–on the
ian Trail!

How inspiring it is to walk all day in the sunshine and sleep all night under the stars.

–Mildred Norman Ryder, first woman to hike the entire Appalachian Trail in no more than 12 months (1908–81)

Convert to metric on p. 170

Talk the Walk:
Learn AT terms
on p. 110.

HIKING THROU

1921

In an article titled "An Appalachian Trail: A Project in Regional Planning," Benton MacKaye proposes establishment of the AT. Benton loved to hike. As an employee of the U.S. Forestry Service and cofounder of The Wilderness Society, he built trails to encourage others to get out and do so, too.

1923

Work begins on a section of the AT in New York state.

1925

Benton organizes the first Appalachian Trail Conference, now known as the Appalachian Trail Conservancy (ATC). The organization continues to protect and manage the trail today.

1931

Myron Avery becomes the leader of the ATC and oversees much of the AT's construction. Over the course of 16 years, he measures every inch of the trail with a measuring wheel, becoming the first person to hike the entire trail.

1937

Trails become fully connected from Georgia to Maine.

1948

Twenty-nine-year-old Earl Schaffer, a World War II veteran, becomes the first thru-hiker, completing his journey from Georgia to Maine in 4 months. The leather boots from his first AT hike are on display at the Smithsonian National Museum of American History.

Earl hikes the trail twice more: once in 1965 and then again in 1998 at age 79.

1952

Mildred Norman Ryder becomes the first female thru-hiker. She and a friend hike from Georgia to Pennsylvania's Susquehanna River, take a bus to Maine, then hike back to the Susquehanna, becoming the first "flip-flop" hikers. (See p. 111.)

1953

At home in Ohio, Emma "Grandma" Gatewood reads an article about the AT and learns that no woman has solo-hiked the trail. The 65-year-old decides to change that. Telling her 11 adult children that she is "going for a hike in the woods," she flies to Maine, but after a few days on the trail, she breaks her glasses and gets lost. Park rangers rescue her and advise her to go home.

GH THE YEARS

1955

Emma, now 67, tries again, this time starting in Georgia on May 3. She carries a homemade backpack and a few supplies but does not take a sleeping bag, tent, compass, or map. She finishes her hike on September 25, averaging 14 miles a day, and becomes the first woman to hike the entire trail alone.

1957

Emma hikes the AT again, becoming the first person to thru-hike it twice.

1968

President Lyndon Johnson signs the National Trails System Act, making the AT a national scenic trail.

1990

Accompanied by Orient, his German shepherd guide dog, Bill Irwin becomes the first blind person to hike the AT. The pair become known as "The Orient Express." Near the end of their hike, the Appalachian Mountain Club gives Bill a two-way radio as a safety measure. For the last 3 weeks, a friend joins them for trekking through the snow and ice. (See p. 111.)

2020

Four-year-old Juniper Netteburg, trail-named "The Beast," completes the trail with her three older siblings and parents in October. After having hiked various sections of the entire trail over 7 months, she becomes one of the youngest people ever to thru-hike the AT.

2021

On August 10, 5-year-old Harvey Sutton completes the AT with his parents.

They began their 209-day journey in January, when Harvey, known as "Little Man" along the trail, was 4. "I would do it again because I like it so much," Harvey says.

On November 7, 2021, 83-year-old M. J. "Eb" Eberhart becomes the oldest person to complete the AT. With his long gray hair and beard, he earns the trail name "Nimblewill Nomad." "The old man on the mountain has got to have a beard," he reasoned. ("Nimblewill Nomad" and "Little Man" did meet up on the trail, where Harvey "impressed the dickens out of me," reported Eb.)

TRAIL TALK

THRU-HIKERS: Folks who hike the entire AT in no more than 12 months

FLIP-FLOP HIKERS: Hikers who don't hike the trail in one continuous route. For instance, instead of hiking from Georgia to Maine, they may start in Virginia, hike to Maine, and then return to Virginia and hike to Georgia.

SECTION HIKERS: Trekkers who hike the trail in pieces, sometimes over a number of years

HIKERS' TRAIL NAMES: Hikers usually choose or are given a hiking nickname. In 2002, hiker Bruce Nichols was called "Birdman" because he often folded origami cranes and gave them to other hikers he met along the way.

RESUPPLY: Many hikers leave the trail from time to time to get food and supplies in nearby towns, so before starting their hikes, some mail packages to themselves to be picked up at post offices along the way.

MAHOOSUC NOTCH: A section of the trail in Maine with a reputation as the AT's longest, toughest mile. Largely flat, it's an obstacle course of huge boulders that hikers have to clamber over, under, and around.

TRAIL DAYS: An annual event held in Damascus, Virginia, on the weekend after Mother's Day to celebrate AT hikers.

BILL IRWIN'S EXCEPTIONAL ADVENTURE

"My boots took a harder beating than most hikers'," the blind hiker reported. "Since I could not see where I was putting my feet, sharp rocks, streams, and weather conditions helped to wear out seven pairs of boots." Bill used a ski pole for balance but ended up breaking six poles and three backpack frames during his hike. His dog Orient carried his own backpack with dog food.

Bill didn't use an AT guidebook or maps to find his way. Instead, he followed detailed instructions on audiotapes that his son and an ATC staff member had made. Sometimes, Bill could use his fingers to read words carved into the wood of trail signs. By about halfway through the hike, Bill became convinced that Orient had learned to recognize the white blazes painted on trees to guide hikers along the AT. When they got off the trail, Orient used the scent of other hikers to lead Bill back to it. At times when they couldn't find their way, Bill would blow a whistle and passing hikers would come to their aid.

MILDRED NORMAN RYDER
MAKES THE MOST OF IT

"I lived out-of-doors completely, supplied with only one pair of slacks and shorts, one blouse and sweater, a lightweight blanket, and two double plastic sheets, into which I sometimes stuffed leaves [as bedding fill]. I was not always completely dry and warm, but I enjoyed it thoroughly." Mildred recalled. "My menu, morning and evening, was 2 cups of uncooked oatmeal soaked in water and flavored with brown sugar; at noon, 2 cups of double-strength dried milk, plus any berries, nuts, or greens found in the woods."

CHANGING THE WORLD,

Do you have a talent that you can share with the world? Or an idea for how to improve it? It's never too early to put your plan into action!

ARTFUL GIFT-GIVER

"Whether I'm happy or sad, art is always there for me," says Chelsea Phaire of Connecticut. In 2019, when she was given a particularly nice art set, her mother told her to take good care of it because many kids don't have art supplies.

This made Chelsea so sad that for her 10th birthday party, she asked guests to bring art supplies instead of gifts. She organized these supplies into 40 art kits and then delivered them to a homeless shelter. After seeing how happy kids were to receive these, Chelsea decided to continue her efforts.

Chelsea's parents helped her to create a nonprofit organization called Chelsea's Charity. She created a wish list of needed items on Amazon so that people could go there to donate them to her cause. Her younger brother, Corey, sometimes helps her to assemble the kits, which are then sent to shelters, foster care agencies, hospitals, and schools. When Chelsea is able to deliver her kits in person, she often gives art lessons to the recipients.

"You're never too old and you're never too young to make a big impact in the world," observes Chelsea. So far, Chelsea's Charity has distributed 20,000 art kits to kids in 47 states and several different countries.

ONE KID AT A TIME

HEARING AID HERO

Braden Baker of Texas was born with hearing loss and has been wearing hearing aids since he was 3 months old. "I kind of like it," says Braden. "It's fun to have something unique about yourself. It makes you feel special."

His dog, Chewy, also liked Braden's hearing aids—so much so, in fact, that he chewed them up not once, but twice! Braden's parents were not amused and explained to then–10-year-old Braden that the devices were expensive. This discussion made Braden wonder what people did when they needed a new pair but didn't have enough money to get them. After some research, Braden made a video to inform people about the problem and asked for donations, eventually raising over $100,000 to help those who couldn't afford hearing aids or replacements.

Braden has continued his efforts with local community groups, a nearby hospital, and several hearing aid companies. He has traveled with hearing aid specialists to Guatemala, Ecuador, and Zambia to help conduct hearing tests and to distribute hearing aids. "I'm happy that I'm able to be part of an amazing community that helps others who need hearing aids all around the world," he says.

Braden encourages other kids to "find your purpose and do something with it."

COLORFUL CREATOR

"I want everybody to know that they can be great," proclaims Taylor "Lola" Thomas of Maryland.

Lola—who uses a wheelchair because she was born with spina bifida—is usually a happy, energetic student. However, at age 8, she was going through a difficult time. Not only was she being bullied at school, but also the coronavirus pandemic was keeping her from one of her favorite activities: having her nails painted at the nail salon.

Determined to find a solution, Lola asked her mother if she could make her own nail polish. With her mom's approval, she not only made her own product but also went on to create her own business, Lola Marie Polish. Her brand, which includes more than 40 colors (all with empowering and positive names) and has been wildly successful, is available through a major retail chain. Lola donates 20 percent of the profits to the Casey Cares Foundation, which helps families of critically ill children. Her sales have also allowed her family to purchase a wheelchair-accessible van.

Lola has more big dreams: Someday, she hopes to take 100 kids in wheelchairs to Disney World.

BULLY BUSTER

"I was bullied a lot," remembers Samirah Horton of New York. Even now, this teenager is sometimes still bullied because of her deep, raspy voice. But Samirah has made her voice her superpower. She's been rapping and DJing since age 6 and has written a song called "No, You Won't Bully Me," as well as a book, *The Bully Stop.*

Calling herself DJ Annie Red, she travels around the country, urging kids to stand up to bullying and reassuring those who have been bullied that they are not alone.

She also performs at a variety of events, including Brooklyn Nets basketball games, where she is the "kid resident DJ."

Inspired by her DJ dad, Samirah took lessons at Scratch Academy in Manhattan. She took her DJ name from her nickname—Annie Red Little Peg—because her face was sometimes red when she was little and she looks just like her grandmother, whose name is Peggy.

Samirah hopes that by telling others how she "took back her power," they will follow her example.

COMMUNITY ENTREPRENEUR

Obocho Peters was a shy kid from New York who sometimes had panic attacks before speaking in public. Today—as a business owner and the youngest member of his local chamber of commerce—he has more than overcome these jitters.

Obocho's transformation started when he saw a superhero movie and asked for several spinoff toys. When his mother said that they couldn't afford them, he decided to earn money to buy them by selling some of his old clothes at a thrift store. Then he had an idea: What if he could help other kids and families to learn how to earn money, too—as well as create savings? This led him to create an online thrift shop that sells donated children's clothes.

"I was inspired by all of the superheroes helping to make the world a better place," Obocho recalls. "I wanted to be a hero myself by helping my mom."

Obocho's mother helped him to build a Web site and signed him up for some business classes. Their home soon began filling up with donations. In 2019, the fifth grader opened a physical store called "Obocho's Closet." Obocho uses a percentage of his business's profits to provide free classes in financial planning, entrepreneurship, and how to save money for college to people of all ages. He and his mom have now also started a neighborhood food pantry.

MUSIC MARVELS

An old joke asks, "How do you get to Carnegie Hall?"—referring to the world-famous concert hall in New York City. The answer? "Practice, practice, practice!" As musical prodigies with jaw-dropping talent, these kids do that and more.

MAKE WAY FOR MARIACHI

As a baby, Mateo Lopez would twirl his feet in his car seat whenever he heard music. As soon as he could talk, the Texas boy began memorizing the words to mariachi songs, a type of Mexican folk music. He began performing at age 4, and by the time he was 7, he had set a world record for being the youngest mariachi singer. He is following in the footsteps of his late grandfather, who was also a mariachi singer. "I love mariachi music because it represents Mexico," Mateo proudly states.

Mateo started guitar and singing lessons when he was 4 and subsequently added piano and harp to his repertoire. He has performed on television shows in the United States, Mexico, and Italy. His mother says that she is incredibly proud of him for "really embracing his culture, embracing the music, and just sharing it with the world."

move over, mozart!

Astounding, brilliant, extraordinary—these are just some of the adjectives used to describe Alma Deutscher's musical talent. A violinist, pianist, conductor, and composer, she has been called "a new Mozart," although Alma rolls her eyes at this comparison.

Born in 2005 and raised in England, she and her family now live in Austria. Alma began playing the piano when she was 2. By age 3, she was playing violin and composing. She says that her songs came from an imaginary world called Transylvanian. Alma had written a piano sonata by the time she was 6 and a short opera by the next year. By age 12, she had composed a full-length Cinderella-based opera; at 14, she made her Carnegie Hall debut.

Alma explains that compositions just pop into her head "when I'm not concentrating, when I'm skipping outside, when I'm falling asleep or just waking up, or while I'm improvising at the piano, when I feel that melodies are going to burst out of my fingertips and I have to hold them in—and then the hard work is sitting down and developing them."

Someday, she hopes to write a symphony. She was inspired by a novel about Mozart's sister, Maria Anna, who secretly wrote symphonies but wasn't taken seriously because she was a girl. "I'm a very strong feminist," Alma notes, "and I'm really happy that I was born now, when girls are allowed to develop their talents."

a one-man band

Neil Nayyar of California has broken two world records for having the ability to play the greatest number of instruments—which for him means the flute, piano, saxophone, harp, and *many* others. In fact, he's adept with 117 instruments from around the world, including the Australian didgeridoo and the Scottish bagpipes, and he wants to learn more. "There are about 4,000 extinct instruments," the enthusiastic teenager says, while noting that he is still researching the subject.

Neil's musical journey started slowly. He had no interest in the drums that his parents offered him when he was 2, but when he tried them again at age 6 during a music class, he quickly caught on. His parents then gave him a guitar, and his musical mindset was launched! Soon he began collecting different instruments, and by age 12, he could play 44. His musical interests include classical, Bollywood, jazz, and rock. He practices 6 to 8 hours a day and has learned from more than 100 teachers.

At sporting events, Neil has even been known to play "The Star-Spangled Banner" on the sitar—a stringed instrument from India.

"I am happiest when I'm playing music," he reports. "It's what helps me to connect with people. My favorite part of learning new instruments is understanding the culture that comes with them."

DRUM ROLL, PLEASE!

When Nandi Bushell plays the drums, she twirls her drumsticks, smiles, and screams, throwing herself into her music. She became a global rock and roll sensation at age 10 and has even had the opportunity to play with some of her musical heroes.

Born in South Africa (she's half Zulu), Nandi now lives in England. When she was a toddler, she "connected" with the Beatles' "Hey Jude"—and especially Ringo Starr on drums. By age 5, she had graduated from toy drums to real drums. Her father recalls: "She instantly kept a beat going with perfect timing. I could not believe what I was hearing." Nandi and her dad posted videos of her playing on social media.

Dave Grohl from the band Foo Fighters saw one of her videos and was impressed. In 2020, 10-year-old Nandi challenged him to a drum-off. He declared her the winner, and their dueling videos attracted millions of viewers. In 2021, he invited Nandi to perform onstage with the band in Los Angeles.

Nandi also plays guitar and saxophone and is learning more instruments. She writes her own songs, too, in between playing music and doing schoolwork. "I just want to have fun and enjoy the journey," she muses, "wherever it may take me."

a Banjo on Her Knee

There's not much music in my family," says Nora Brown, a New York City resident who nonetheless has become a banjo sensation. She started with ukulele lessons, and when she was 6, she began taking lessons with the late Shlomo Pestcoe, a well-known performer and teacher who specialized in traditional music.

"Shlomo would have us play these recital-like things, which he called a 'hootenanny,'" Nora recalls. "I learned that it was not a scary thing to perform and that it was important to share music."

Eventually, she took up the banjo and started learning from seasoned musicians like master banjo player Lee Sexton, a former coal miner from Kentucky. As the pair would sit down and share songs and stories, her initial nervousness would turn into a feeling of comfort and security. Nora says that such experiences "completely changed my relationship with the music that I play."

Inspired by the old-time music of eastern Kentucky and Tennessee, she released her first album, *Cinnamon Tree*—which debuted in the Top 10 of the *Billboard* Bluegrass Chart—when she was 13. At 16, she recorded her second album, *Sidetrack My Engine*, in an unusual spot: the caves and tunnels underneath her parents' cheese shop. One reviewer described her music as "some of the most interesting and haunting traditional music that we've heard."

Not surprisingly, Nora has won many banjo and folk song competitions—and many more honors are no doubt yet to come.

Insect I Spy

How many of each insect are
floating around? Count them up and fill in
the answers in the circles below.

FIND

ANSWERS: 1 = 5, 2 = 1, 3 = 5, 4 = 5, 5 = 8, 6 = 4, 7 = 4, 8 = 4, 9 = 4, 10 = 4.

Incredible Ice

In 2018, a 14,400-year-old piece of bread was found at an excavation site in Jordan.

The earliest written recipe for "icy cream" was found in a 1665 cookbook.

FOOD

It takes 3 gallons of milk to make 1 gallon of ice cream.

Cream Bread

How many baking recipes do you know that require only two ingredients? If you answered "none," get ready to learn about an incredibly versatile and tasty one! You need just two ingredients to make this bread— and it gets better: One of the ingredients is ice cream! Honest. Cookies and cream bread? *Yes!* Maple walnut bread? *Yes!* Black raspberry chocolate chip bread? *Yes!* The choice is *yours,* and we encourage experimenting.

YOU WILL NEED:

loaf pan
nonstick cooking spray
bowl
spoon
cooling rack
2 cups of your favorite ice cream (not dairy-free), softened
1½ cups self-rising flour
sprinkles (also called "jimmies"), optional

Convert to metric on p. 170

1. Preheat the oven to 350°F.

2. Coat the loaf pan with nonstick cooking spray. Set aside.

3. Put the ice cream into the bowl and stir until very smooth and melty. (The more melted the ice cream is, the easier it will mix with the flour.)

4. Add the flour and stir just until combined.

5. Pour into prepared pan and cover with sprinkles (if using).

6. Bake for 40 to 45 minutes, or until a tester (such as a toothpick or uncooked piece of spaghetti) inserted into the middle of the bread comes out clean.

7. Allow bread to cool slightly, then turn out onto a cooling rack.

Makes 1 loaf.

The first pre-sliced bread appeared on shelves in Chillicothe, Missouri, in 1928.

SAY "CHEEEE

 Has a friend ever said this when taking your pic? (Or maybe you've heard it a *million* times!)

The expression first appeared in a Texas newspaper in the 1940s, but no one is certain who came up with the idea of using it to make people smile. The word "cheese" was likely chosen because both the "ch" and "ee" sounds require us to show our teeth, resulting in a wide grin. Try it!

But there's much more to cheese than smiling—even though a yummy grilled cheese sandwich might make you do just that.

Although it usually comes from cow's milk, cheese can also be made from the milk of sheep, goats, donkeys, moose, water buffalo, reindeer, camels, and yaks.

Cheese may have been discovered accidentally when milk was stored in containers made from the stomachs of animals such as cows, sheep, and goats. Rennet, an enzyme found there, causes milk to thicken and separate into curds (solids) and whey (liquid).

Some archaeologists have found cheese-

Why didn't the cheese want to get sliced? It had grater plans!

EEEEESE"!

making tools that date back at least 7,000 years. Evidence of cheese and cheese-making has been found buried with Egyptian mummies and painted on murals in tombs, and making cheese is mentioned in ancient Greek mythology. Ancient Romans used cheese as currency.

Closer to home . . .

■ THE PILGRIMS brought cheese with them when they arrived in America in 1620.

■ THE FIRST CHEESE factory in the U.S. was built in 1851 in Oneida County, New York.

■ WHEN SWISS immigrants settled in Green County, Wisconsin, they began to manufacture foreign cheeses. The first "stinky" cheese (Limburger) factory opened in 1868.

■ WISCONSIN MAKES one-quarter of all of the cheese in the United States.

■ CANADA'S FIRST cheese factory, The Pioneer, was started in Norwich, Ontario, in 1864.

■ AT ONE POINT in the early 1900s, there were 1,242 cheddar cheese factories in the province of Ontario, as cheddar became one of Canada's biggest exports of any type.

HOW IS CHEESE MADE?

Most cheese is made with just three ingredients: milk, salt, and some type of hardener, such as rennet, vinegar, or bacteria. The milk is heated until it starts to separate, or curdle. The whey is removed, and the curds are tightly packed into large molds that are often in the shape of a wheel. The cheese is dried and preserved, or cured, until it is firm enough to be removed from the mold and stored on racks in climate-controlled rooms to finish curing.

Some cheeses are ready in only a few weeks or months, while others can take years to cure! A wheel may be covered in wax or loosely wrapped in cheese-cloth. As cheese cures, it forms a rind on its exterior. If the rind is not easily edible, it is removed before eating.

HEY, WHEY?

Whey is the thin liquid left over after cheese-making. It contains protein and lactose (milk sugar). Whey is used to make ricotta cheese and is added to many protein bars.

Little Miss Muffet
Sat on a tuffet,
Eating her curds and whey;
Along came a spider,
Who sat down beside her,
And frightened Miss Muffet away.
-Mother Goose poem

PROTEIN BAR

CHEESE BITES

- There are more than 1,800 different cheese varieties in the world.
- Mozzarella is the most popular cheese in the United States.
- It takes 10 pounds of milk to make 1 pound of cheese.
- The holes in Swiss cheese are the result of little air pockets made by carbon dioxide given off by bacteria in the cheese.
- Big cheese wheels are easily moved by rolling.
- A giant wheel of cheddar cheese weighing more than 1,000 pounds was given to Queen Victoria (1819–1901) as a wedding gift.
- The most expensive cheese in the world is Pule donkey cheese. It's made only in Serbia and costs about $600 for 1 pound.

LOCAL CHEESE

Some cheese names come from names of the towns or locations where they were first made:

- Cheddar cheese, which dates back to the 12th century, is named after a small town in southwestern England.
- Colby cheese is named after a town in Wisconsin.
- Havarthigaard, a family farm in Denmark, gave Havarti cheese its name.

What kind of cheese is made backward?
Edam!
[a type of Dutch cheese]

CHEESE OF A DIFFERENT COLOR

Orange cheese is a tradition that goes back hundreds of years. Cheddar cheese in England was once made with milk from cows whose beta carotene-rich diet (think carrots) produced orange-tinted milk. Today, orange cheeses are colored with annatto, the fruit of the achiote tree.

Blue cheese is made from milk with the harmless mold *Penicillium* added. This mold creates streaks of blue inside the cheese as it cures and gives it a sharp, salty flavor. Certain other bacteria that are added give the blue cheese a strong odor. Blue cheese is thought to have been invented by accident hundreds of years ago when cheeses were cured in caves, where the environment was cool and moist. Molds in these caves made their way into the cheeses.

WATER BUFFALO CHEESE

Mozzarella cheese was first made in southern Italy from the rich milk of water buffalo. Fresh *mozzarella di bufala* is still a delicacy around the world. The name "mozzarella" comes from the Italian word *mozzare*, which refers to the way in which the cheese curd is stretched in strips and then cut. Today, the cheese is made mainly from cow's milk.

EXTRA CHEESE

WHAT IS COTTAGE CHEESE?

Cottage cheese is a fresh, mild-tasting, low-fat, protein-rich cheese made by cutting the curds into small pieces and mixing them with whey or cream. Its name came about because farmers would use leftover milk to make it in their small homes, or "cottages."

WHAT IS CREAM CHEESE?

Cream cheese is a fresh, soft, mild-tasting cheese made from a mix of cream and milk. It is available plain, as well as flavored with herbs, fruit, vegetables, meat, or fish.

Knock, knock.
Who's there?
Cheese!
Cheese who?
Cheese a jolly good fellow!

WHO PUT THE "JACK" IN MONTEREY CHEESE?

In the late 1700s, Spanish Franciscan missionaries at Monterey Bay, California, created a mild white cheese called *queso blanco pais*. In 1859, David Jack bought most of the land and farms in Monterey and started selling the locally made cheese as Jack's Cheese. Soon the cheese was sold across California and other states as Monterey Jack's Cheese.

Convert to metric on p. 170

EASY HOMEMADE MACARONI AND CHEESE

With an adult's help, you can make this favorite cheesy pasta dish.

YOU WILL NEED:

13x9-inch baking dish
nonstick cooking spray
pot
skillet
spoon

whisk
1 1/2 cups elbow macaroni
1/4 cup (1/2 stick) butter
1/2 teaspoon salt
dash of freshly ground
   black pepper

1/4 cup all-purpose flour
1 3/4 cups milk
1 cup shredded cheese
   (choose your favorite
   kind)

1. Preheat the oven to 350°F.

2. Spray the baking dish with nonstick cooking spray.

3. In the pot, cook macaroni according to package directions.

4. In the skillet over low heat, melt the butter.

5. Add salt and pepper and stir.

6. Add flour and cook, stirring constantly for 1 minute.

7. Add milk and use the whisk to combine.

8. Add cheese and stir until it melts.

9. Drain macaroni and pour into the prepared dish.

10. Pour cheese mixture over the macaroni and stir to combine.

11. Bake for 30 minutes, or until golden brown.

Makes 4 servings.

A CHEESY MAZE

(Hint: There's more than one route to the exit!)

FINISH

START

(SAMPLE SOLUTION ON PAGE 171.)

María Orosa's

Meet the culinary adventurer, chemist, inventor, and war heroine who developed more than 700 recipes.

Filipina scientist María Ylagan Orosa was always thinking about new ways to do things, especially when it came to food. During her lifetime, the Philippines struggled for independence. María wanted to make her country less dependent on other nations for food, so she found new ways to use local crops.

In the Beginning

María Orosa was born on November 29, 1893, in the Philippine town of Taal. In school, María's favorite subject was science. After studying for a year at the University of the Philippines, she won a scholarship to attend the University of Seattle in Washington state. At age 23, she worked aboard a ship to pay for passage to the United States. At the university, she earned degrees in food chemistry, pharmaceutical chemistry, and pharmacy.

To support herself while in school, she washed dishes, mopped floors, and picked fruit. In summer, María worked at salmon canneries in Alaska, where she learned about preserving and packaging food. She also worked as an assistant chemist at the University of Washington, testing food samples for state inspectors.

Filipina Food Pioneer

María returned to the Philippines after university, determined to fight the problem of hunger and scarce food supplies. She became a chemist for the Philippine Bureau of Science and experimented with different ways to can, dehydrate, ferment, and freeze local

Edible Inventions

produce. María made jellies from guava, mango, and other tropical fruit. She was the first to freeze and can mangoes, which meant that they could be shipped around the world.

María started clubs in the Philippines to teach new ways to raise poultry, preserve food, and prepare inexpensive, healthy meals. By 1924, the overall organization had over 22,000 members. She invented a type of clay oven that could be used with two pieces of metal to bake over an open fire. This was especially useful in villages without electricity. She traveled extensively, demonstrating her ideas and learning new ones; in 1926, she visited more than 50 canneries in the United States, Europe, China, and Japan to learn more about food processing. In 1927, she was appointed director of the Philippines' newly created Division of Food Preservation.

María to the Rescue!

When World War II broke out in 1939, food shortages became common everywhere. María developed a powdered soybean product nicknamed "magic food" because it contained so many nutrients. She also made cookies out of rice flour that provided vitamin B_1, an important vitamin for good health.

After Japanese troops invaded the Philippines, María found ways to get "magic food" and rice cookies into camps where Filipinos and Americans were being held as prisoners of war. These prisoners might have starved without María's help. Her relatives have heard many people say, "My grandfather survived the war because of María Y. Orosa."

During this time, tomatoes for ketchup were in short supply, so María came up with a recipe that used . . . bananas! See the next page to try it yourself. The concoction remains a popular staple in Philippine cuisine.

Memories of María

A street in Manila has been named in her honor, and a commemorative marker reminds passersby of her legacy. Her recipes are available in the book *Appetite for Freedom: The Recipes of María Y. Orosa* (Ige Ramos Design Studio, 2021).

Banana Ketchup

YOU WILL NEED:
saucepan
wooden spoon
jar with a lid
2 tablespoons vegetable
  or canola oil
2 cloves garlic, minced

½ cup chopped onion
1 tablespoon minced
  ginger
½ teaspoon turmeric
½ teaspoon ground
  allspice
1 tablespoon tomato paste

4 ripe bananas, mashed
½ cup brown sugar
½ cup white vinegar
2 tablespoons soy sauce
  or coconut aminos
red food coloring
  (optional)

1. In the saucepan over medium-low heat, warm the oil.

2. Add the garlic and onions and cook, stirring often, for 5 minutes.

3. Add the ginger, turmeric, and allspice. Continuously stir the
  mixture and cook for 1 minute.

4. Add the tomato paste and cook, stirring often, for 5 minutes,
  or until onions start to turn golden.

5. Add bananas, brown sugar, vinegar, and soy sauce. Stir well, reduce
  heat to low, and cook for 10 minutes, or until mixture thickens.
  (If you wish to make this look more like traditional ketchup, stir in
  a few drops of red food coloring once the mixture has thickened.)
  Set aside to cool.

6. Transfer ketchup to the jar, cover, and store in the refrigerator for
  up to 2 weeks.

Convert
to metric
on p. 170

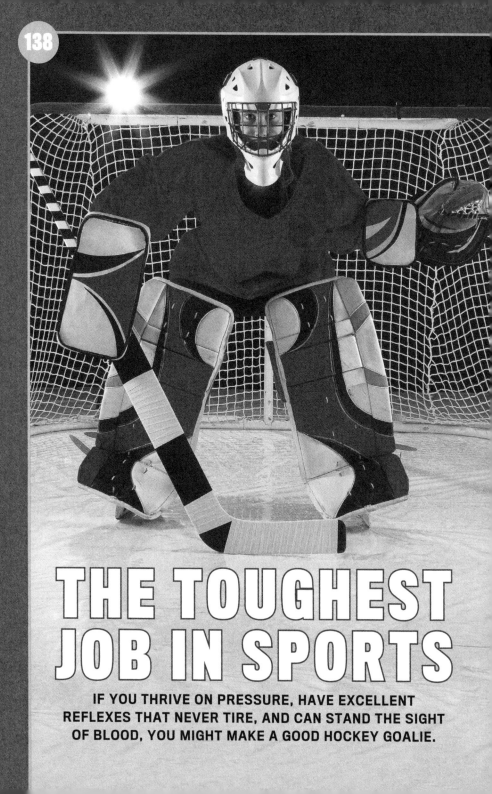

THE TOUGHEST JOB IN SPORTS

IF YOU THRIVE ON PRESSURE, HAVE EXCELLENT
REFLEXES THAT NEVER TIRE, AND CAN STAND THE SIGHT
OF BLOOD, YOU MIGHT MAKE A GOOD HOCKEY GOALIE.

The ice hockey goal seems like an innocent place in the moments before a game. Seconds before the opening face-off at center ice, the goalie skates over to the net, pivots, and crouches. The moment the referee drops the puck and the game begins, the goalie's home becomes a target.

JOB REQUIREMENTS

The goalie's job is to patrol the "crease," a designated area in front of the net, and stop the puck (a 5.5- to 6-ounce, 1-inch-thick, black disk of vulcanized rubber) as it hurtles toward the net, sometimes reaching speeds of more than 100 miles per hour. Dunc Wilson, a National Hockey League (NHL) goalie for 10 seasons, compared being hit by a puck to being struck by a sledgehammer. During one game, he took the first shot squarely on his mask—and it knocked him out!

DRESS CODE

No athlete in any sport goes into a game so well protected. Thick pads cover the goalie's legs. A chest protector and elbow and shoulder pads beneath the jersey swell the goalie's size, bringing to mind the Stay Puft Marshmallow Man. On one hand, the goalie wears a flexible "catching" mitt for snaring pucks; on the other, a stiff, heavy "blocking glove" with which both to hold the extra-wide goalie stick and to deflect inbound pucks on that side. The throat is protected by a special collar or a polycarbonate shield that dangles from a mask attached to a fiberglass or Kevlar helmet. The goalie's face is protected by a stainless steel cage built to withstand the force of pucks slamming into it—as well as deflect slower ones. Former Boston Bruins coach Don Cherry spoke for all who have ever guarded the net when he said, "There is no such thing as painless goaltending."

FACE OFF!

For years, goalies didn't wear face masks during games. Clint Benedict of the Montreal Maroons was the first pro to wear one, in 1930, but they didn't catch on. In 1956, Jacques Plante began wearing a mask during Montreal Canadiens practices, but his coach, Toe Blake, forbade him to wear it during a game. Coach Blake thought that the mask signified weakness. Of course, he was a former forward and had never been on the receiving end of a slap shot. On November 1, 1959, Jacques took a puck to the face for what was to be the last time. In the dressing room, where cuts on his face were being stitched up, he told Coach Blake that he would not play again without some face protection. Coach Blake finally agreed, and Jacques began wearing a mask.

At a practice during the 1968–69 season, a puck hit the face mask of then–Boston Bruins goalie Gerry Cheevers. Team trainer John "Frosty" Forristall came up with an idea to show just how valuable masks really were. After every game, Frosty painted stitch or scar marks on Gerry's mask to indicate where the goalie had been newly struck by a puck or stick. For the remainder of his career, Gerry wore the same, increasingly marked-up mask, with a new "stitch" added after every time that it was hit.

In 1974, Andy Brown of the Pittsburgh Penguins became the last NHL goalie to play without a mask.

CLINT BENEDICT   JACQUES PLANTE   GERRY CHEEVERS

UNDER PRESSURE

Playing injuries are only part of the hockey goalie's story. The outcome of a game can rest almost entirely on the shoulders of the goalie, which means that the pressure involved can be overwhelming. Consider the career of Frank McCool. Named NHL rookie of the year in 1945, Frank recorded three straight shutouts (no goals allowed) while leading the Toronto Maple Leafs to the 1945 Stanley Cup championship. Yet he played only 2 years. Almost every time that he took the ice, he became nearly doubled over from stomach pain due to stress.

FRANK McCOOL

Glenn Hall's record 502 consecutive regular season NHL games earned him the nickname "Mr. Goalie," but he was also famous for his nervous stomach. He felt sick so often before and during games that he kept a spit bucket at his team's bench and sipped a stomach-soothing tea between periods. Glenn didn't worry about this, though, once saying, "Nervousness was part of the game—it helped to keep me sharp."

SPORTS SEARCH

Find the sports words hidden in the puzzle.

V	T	A	B	L	E	T	E	N	N	I	S	S	X
W	J	U	D	O	Q	T	I	R	O	W	I	N	G
A	U	B	A	S	K	E	T	B	A	L	L	E	G
R	U	G	B	Y	A	N	B	A	T	C	K	A	Y
I	H	U	G	K	Y	N	U	S	H	Y	S	C	M
M	F	R	B	J	U	I	G	E	L	C	U	R	N
G	O	L	F	R	G	S	D	B	E	L	R	I	A
B	O	X	I	N	G	X	I	A	T	I	F	C	S
I	T	O	G	C	A	R	D	L	I	N	I	K	T
N	B	H	O	C	K	E	Y	L	C	G	N	E	I
B	A	D	M	I	N	T	O	N	S	E	G	T	C
B	L	P	V	O	L	L	E	Y	B	A	L	L	S
K	L	Y	L	F	S	K	A	T	I	N	G	U	L
N	P	S	S	W	I	M	M	I	N	G	P	Z	T

ATHLETICS   CRICKET   HOCKEY   SURFING
BADMINTON   CYCLING   JUDO   SWIMMING
BASEBALL   FOOTBALL   ROWING   TABLE TENNIS
BASKETBALL   GOLF   RUGBY   TENNIS
BOXING   GYMNASTICS   SKATING   VOLLEYBALL

(SOLUTION ON PAGE 171.)

Are you ready for an afternoon of friendly competition? Prepare for hours of backyard fun that will include grass stains, near misses, and highlight reel catches!

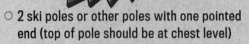

YOU WILL NEED:

- 2 ski poles or other poles with one pointed end (top of pole should be at chest level)
- 1 Frisbee (also known as a flying disc)
- 2 empty bottles—metal, hard plastic, or glass (check with an adult if using glass)
- 4 players

HOW TO SET UP:

- Find a flat, grassy playing area.
- Place your poles anywhere from 20 to 40 feet apart. Push the pointed end of each pole into the ground so that the pole stays straight up and stands on its own.
- Balance one bottle on top of each pole.

HOW TO PLAY:

- The goal of the game is to knock the bottle off of the other team's pole by hitting either the bottle or the pole with the disc.
- Divide into two teams and choose which team will go first.
- Each team stands slightly behind one of the poles.
- The first player throws the disc in an attempt to knock the bottle off the other team's pole.
- Next, a player from the opposite team throws the disc back in an attempt to knock down the bottle on the other team's pole. After the remaining two players alternate throws, continue to follow the same throwing pattern.
- Once each thrown disc is past its target pole, players on the opposing team attempt to catch it.
- Continue trying to knock down the bottles in alternating turns until a score of 11 is reached.

HOW TO KEEP SCORE:

○ **2 points** = Disc hits the bottle directly, knocking it off the pole.

○ **1 point** = Disc hits the pole, not the bottle, but knocks the bottle off the pole.

○ **1 point** = Receiving team catches the disc.

BASIC RULES:

○ The disc can not hit the ground in front of the pole. If it does and then hits the pole, knocking the bottle off, no points are awarded.

○ Players can not interfere with a throw by catching the disc in front of the pole or blocking the pole in any way. If such interference is called, 2 points are awarded to the throwing team.

FIRST FRISBEE

The origin of the flying disc dates back to 1871, when college students in Bridgeport, Connecticut, would throw empty pie tins from the Frisbie Pie Company to each other. They would yell "Frisbie!" as they let go.

In 1948, Walter "Fred" Morrison and Warren Franscioni invented the "Flyin' Saucer," an improved plastic version of the original tin pie plates that could fly farther and with more accuracy. Fred upgraded the saucer and renamed it the "Pluto Platter." He sold them at county fairs and in parking lots, where he was discovered by a representative from Wham-O toy company.

Wham-O bought the invention from Fred in 1957, and the first batch of saucers—then known as aerodynamic plastic discs—was soon released. Wham-O renamed the toy "Frisbee."

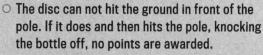

Unwind Your Mind

GAMES · SPORTS · HOMEWORK · CHORES · PATIENCE · BEING ON TIME · LISTENING · KINDNESS

It is sometimes easy to get lost in troubling thoughts and be overwhelmed by the way that your body reacts to being worried or anxious. There are things that you can do to try to calm yourself. Many of these techniques involve focusing on what's happening right now. This is called "being mindful" or "practicing mindfulness." Being mindful helps you to focus and soothe your mind and body so that you can better control how you react to situations.

You can use mindfulness methods when you have a lot on your mind—like thinking about getting your homework done, or how to win at that video game you've been playing, or being on time for soccer practice. Having a busy mind can be distracting, even if the things that you are thinking about are all pleasant. Slowing down and being mindful helps you to put distracting thoughts aside and focus on what is happening at the moment.

Here are some exercises that you can try to get started on your mindful journey.

5-4-3-2-1 Technique

Take a deep breath, then look around and describe out loud . . .

5 objects that you see (such as a pencil, your shoe, or a bird).

4 objects that you can feel or touch (such as your hair, the ground against your feet, or a string).

3 things that you can hear (such as a car going by or the washing machine running).

2 things that you can smell (such as the hand soap that you used or the aroma of baking cookies). If you can't smell anything where you are, say 2 smells that you like.

1 thing that you can taste (such as the mint toothpaste that you brushed with today). If you can't taste anything, say 1 thing that you like to taste.

Take another deep breath.

The S-T-O-P Technique

S: Stop. Pause whatever it is that you are doing.

T: Take a deep breath. Think about this deep breath and take another. You can softly say "in" as you're breathing in and "out" as you're breathing out if it helps you to concentrate.

O: Observe. Notice what is happening inside and outside of your body. What are you feeling? What are you doing?

P: Proceed. Go back to what you were doing. Or don't—maybe this pause made you realize that you need to make a change.

Breathing Technique #1

Sit in a comfortable position or lie on your back on the floor. Close your eyes.
Be aware of your breathing as you inhale and exhale normally. Simply pay attention as your breath goes in and then goes out.

Notice how each breath gently moves your body. Put your hands on your belly or your chest and feel it moving as you breathe.

Stay still for a few minutes, focusing on your gentle breathing. Just as with the S-T-O-P technique, you can softly say "in" as you're breathing in and "out" as you're breathing out if it helps you to concentrate.

If your mind starts to wander and think about other things, guide your attention back to your breathing.

Continue focusing on your breathing until you feel calm.

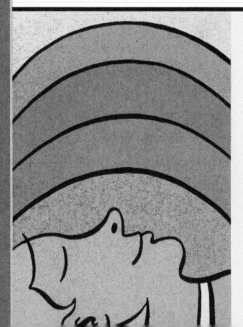

Breathing Technique #2

Sit in a comfortable position or lie on your back on the floor. Close your eyes.

Breathe in and feel the air coming into your nose.

Breathe out as you count 1.

Breathe in and be aware of the air filling your lungs.

Breathe out as you count to 2.

Breathe in and feel the air expanding your belly.

Breathe out as you count to 3.

Repeat two to three more times, until you feel calm and focused.

Talk to a grown-up about finding more exercises to help you to practice mindfulness.

Put Your Head to Bed

Mindful exercises can also help if you're wide awake at bedtime. Try one of the breathing techniques to soothe yourself so that you can calm down and fall asleep.

Be Like Spaghetti

Dr. Ana Maria Verissimo, a doctor dedicated to the health of children, advises us to "be like spaghetti" when overwhelmed or overcome with emotions. Imagine a piece of spaghetti—when it is not cooked, it is stiff. But when spaghetti is cooked, it bends. Dr. Verissimo wants us to be able to bend when things go wrong or we are mad or sad. Think to yourself, "This won't break me."

BRAIN FREEZE!

OH, NO!

You ate your ice cream or slurped your slushy too fast and now you have that excruciating pain in your forehead. A "brain freeze," or "ice cream headache," is painful, but—luckily—it is also brief. A typical brain freeze lasts from a few seconds to 2 minutes. But what exactly is happening?

MEDICALLY SPEAKING,

this agonizing phenomenon is called a cold-stimulus headache, or sphenopalatine ganglioneuralgia (SFEE-no-PAL-uh-teen GAN-glee-o-nyur-AHL-jee-uh). It happens when you eat or drink something very cold and the roof of your mouth cools down quickly. Your body reacts by trying to warm it back up. The blood vessels in the roof of your mouth constrict, or tighten, which sends a signal to your brain to send warmth to the area. The blood vessels then rapidly dilate, or widen, to supply extra blood to the area for warmth. This sudden change initiates a pain signal that results in what is known as "referred pain," which is pain that you feel in a part of your body different from where the signal originated. This is why you feel the severe pain in your forehead and not your mouth. To help relieve the pain, you can press your tongue or thumb to the roof of your mouth to help to warm it up.

ALTHOUGH YOUR BRAIN

is not actually freezing, the pain is real. But the good news is that brain freeze is easy to prevent—just eat or drink cold items more slowly.

Vanilla, chocolate, and strawberry,
  Ice cream makes me merry!
It tastes so good on a really hot day,
  As I lie down lazily in the cool shade.
It's starting to melt, I'd better eat quick,
  But eating so fast is making me sick.
Better slow down and take it with ease,
  But now it's too late! I have a BRAIN FREEZE!

JUST LUCKY, WE GUESS

A study of 8,359 middle school students found that only 41 percent of them had experienced a brain freeze.

WHEN LEFT IS RIGHT

Only around one in 10 people is left-handed. This means that there are probably at least two kids in your class who use their left hand to throw a ball or draw a picture.

There was a time when teachers insisted that all students, including left-handers, learn to write with their right hand. Teachers thought that students would have an easier time if they were not "different" from right-handed writers. Some thought that using the left hand was just a bad habit. Some even punished left-handed kids who had trouble switching to their right hand. Of course, now we know that everyone should use whichever hand is most comfortable because there is no "right"—or correct—hand.

It's not surprising that lefties sometimes feel left out. Consider that . . .

- The Latin word for left, *sinister*, also means unlucky, evil, and suspicious.
- The French word for left, *gauche*, also means clumsy.
- A left-handed compliment is an insult.

Luckily, some cultures have been more kind. The Inca, an old civilization in South America, believed that left-handed people had special spiritual powers. The North American Zuni peoples considered it good luck to be left-handed.

THE LEFT, THE RIGHT, AND THE BRAIN

Scientists aren't sure what causes left-handedness. The genes that you inherit from your parents play a part, but they're not the whole story. For example, identical twins have the same DNA, but it is common for one twin to be right-handed and the other to be left-handed. Many left-handers have a symmetrical brain, meaning that the left and right portions of their brain are shaped alike. Right-handers often have an asymmetrical brain: The left cerebral hemisphere is larger than the right one.

BURGERS FOR LEFTIES

A full-page ad in *USA Today* in 1998 claimed that Burger King had developed the Left-Handed Whopper. The burger had the usual toppings, said the ad, but they were turned 180 degrees so that they wouldn't drip out on left-handed customers. It was all a joke! The ad ran on April 1 (April Fools' Day).

A DAY TO BE LEFT

August 13 is International Left-Handers Day. The tradition was started in 1992 by the Left-Handers Club, a group in the United Kingdom.

BASEBALL BANTER

A left-handed baseball pitcher is called a "south-paw"—and there is no such thing as a "northpaw."

Happy LEFT Handers Day

LEFT-HANDER HEAVEN

Lefties might want to travel to Left Hand, West Virginia, where there is a church, a school, a library, and a post office. The village was named not after the dominant hands of its citizens, but after Left Hand Run, a nearby stream.

WHERE IT'S LUCKY TO BE LEFTY

For a number of years, left-handers who attended Juniata College in Pennsylvania benefited from a scholarship just for left-handers established in 1979 by Mary and Frederick Beckley, two left-handers who met when they attended a tennis class there together in 1919.

TRY YOUR HAND

If you're right-handed, try writing with your left. If you're left-handed, try brushing your teeth with your right. You're likely to find these activities difficult!

WELL-KNOWN LEFTIES

NEIL ARMSTRONG, American astronaut
JUSTIN BIEBER, Canadian singer-songwriter
LEONARDO DA VINCI, Italian artist
ALBERT EINSTEIN, German-born physicist
LADY GAGA, American singer-songwriter
BARACK OBAMA, 44th U.S. president
ZOE SALDAÑA, American actress
PRINCE WILLIAM of Wales
A'JA WILSON, American basketball player
OPRAH WINFREY, American entrepreneur

POPS FOR YOUR PUP

Making healthy treats for your four-legged friend is a fun activity for you and your pet. Here are three different frozen "pupsicles" to get your dog's tail wagging.

BLUEBERRY PUPSICLES

YOU WILL NEED:
blender
ice cube trays
zip-close freezer bag

$1\frac{1}{2}$ cups blueberries
$\frac{2}{3}$ cup canned lite coconut milk
dog bone treats

1. Put blueberries and coconut milk into the blender. Process for 1 to 2 minutes, or until it is the consistency of a smoothie.
2. Pour into ice cube trays, filling about ¾ full.
3. Insert a dog bone treat into each cube.
4. Put into the freezer for 4 hours, or until solid.
5. Remove treats from ice cube trays and place in a zip-close freezer bag.
6. These treats can be stored in the freezer for up to 4 months.

Convert to metric on p. 170

CANDY CORN PUPSICLES

YOU WILL NEED:
spoon
freezer pop molds
zip-close freezer bag
1 cup low-fat plain yogurt (make
  sure that it does not contain
  any artificial sweeteners such
  as xylitol)

1 can (15 ounces) pumpkin
  purée (make sure that it is not
  pumpkin pie filling)
1 large banana, mashed
stick dog treats, carrot sticks,
  or celery sticks

1. Spoon yogurt into the bottom ⅓ of each pop mold.
2. Fill the molds another ⅓ full with pumpkin purée.
3. Top off the molds with mashed bananas, leaving a little space at the top so that they can expand.
4. Insert a dog treat stick into each mold.
5. Put into the freezer for 4 hours, or until solid.
6. Run the molds under warm water for a few seconds to loosen them up, then remove the treats from the molds. Place in a zip-close freezer bag.
7. These treats can be stored in the freezer for up to 4 months.

NOTE: Always be sure to feed your dog its treats under adult supervision and to remember that dogs can not eat everything that you can. Check with your veterinarian.

WATERMELON CARROT PUPSICLES

YOU WILL NEED:
freezer pop molds
blender

zip-close freezer bag
2 medium carrots,
peeled and chopped

3 cups chopped
seedless watermelon

1. Put carrots into the blender. Process until finely chopped.

2. Add watermelon to the blender. Process until watermelon and carrots are smooth.

3. Pour into molds and put into the freezer for 4 hours, or until solid.

4. Remove treats from molds and place in a zip-close freezer bag.

5. These treats can be stored in the freezer for up to 3 months.

THE HASKELL FREE LIBRARY AND OPERA HOUSE IS IN BOTH THE U.S. AND CANADA. THE LIBRARY COLLECTION AND OPERA STAGE ARE IN STANSTEAD, QUEBEC, BUT THE ENTRANCE AND MANY OF THE THEATER SEATS ARE IN DERBY LINE, VERMONT.

AMAZING AND TRUE!

ASTOUND YOUR FRIENDS, FAMILY, AND TEACHERS WITH THESE MIND-BOGGLING FACTS!

Scientists have observed snowfall on Mars.

Lemons float, but limes sink.

IN 1845, PORTLAND, OREGON, GOT ITS NAME IN A "BEST TWO OUT OF THREE" COIN FLIP. IF IT HAD GONE THE OTHER WAY, PORTLAND WOULD HAVE BEEN NAMED "BOSTON."

Under its fur, a polar bear has black skin.

Male cats tend to be left-pawed, while female cats are often right-pawed.

IT TAKES ABOUT 90 DAYS FOR A SINGLE RAINDROP THAT FALLS INTO THE MISSISSIPPI RIVER TO TRAVEL ITS ENTIRE 2,340-MILE-LONG LENGTH.

Cashews, pistachios, and mangoes are related to the poison ivy plant.

Butterflies taste with their feet.

THE LONGEST AMOUNT OF TIME POSSIBLE BETWEEN CONSECUTIVE LEAP YEARS IS 8 YEARS. THE NEXT TIME THIS HAPPENS WILL BE BETWEEN 2096 AND 2104.

The current 50-star U.S. flag was designed by a 17-year-old Ohio high school student as a history project in 1958. (And he got a B– on it!)

During World War II, a bear was enlisted as a private in the Polish Army.

A hummingbird beats its wings about 70 times per second.

WHEN SPELLED OUT, NO WHOLE NUMBER BEFORE 1,000 CONTAINS THE LETTER A.

Find the Forest Dwellers

(SOLUTION ON PAGE 171.)

UNDERCOVER INK

IMAGINE THAT YOU GET A NOTE FROM ONE OF YOUR FRIENDS, BUT WHEN YOU LOOK AT IT, THE PAPER IS BLANK. WHAT HAPPENED TO THE WORDS? YOU JUST RECEIVED A SECRET MESSAGE WRITTEN IN INVISIBLE INK!

ANCIENT GREEKS AND ROMANS were using invisible ink more than 2,000 years ago to send secret messages. Pliny the Elder, a Roman naturalist in the 1st century A.D., discovered that sap from the tithymalus plant disappeared when dried and reappeared when he sprinkled ashes over it.

A TALE OF TWO GEORGES

GENERAL GEORGE WASHINGTON sent and received messages using invisible ink during the Revolutionary War. One of his soldiers created the system, which employed one chemical for writing and another—nicknamed "the medicine"—to make the ink appear.

GEORGE VAUX BACON was an American working as a spy for Germany during World War I. The invisible ink that he used to communicate with the Germans was hidden in his socks! The brown, toothpaste-like substance was spread on top of his black socks, which were later soaked in water to create liquid ink.

JUST LIKE A SECRET AGENT, YOU CAN COMMUNICATE WITH FRIENDS THROUGH MESSAGES IN INVISIBLE INK THAT YOU MAKE YOURSELF.

Convert to metric on p. 170

BAKING SODA INK

Baking soda mixed into water is invisible when applied to white paper. To make it visible, you need to add an acidic solution—in this case, a mixture of rubbing alcohol and the bright yellow spice turmeric.

YOU WILL NEED:
2 small glass bowls
white paper
small paintbrush
medium-size paintbrush
1 tablespoon baking soda
½ cup water
1 teaspoon turmeric
½ cup rubbing alcohol

1. In one bowl, stir the baking soda into the water.

2. Dip the small paintbrush into the baking soda mixture and write a message on the paper. Wait for it to dry.

3. In the other bowl, mix the turmeric into the rubbing alcohol. Be careful, as this mixture can stain your hands or clothes.

4. Use the medium-size paint brush to paint the turmeric mixture over the secret message to make it appear.

LEMON JUICE INK

Lemon juice turns brown when exposed to heat.

YOU WILL NEED: small paintbrush   lamp with   lemon juice
small bowl or jar   or cotton swab   a lightbulb   water
white paper

1. Squeeze or pour a few tablespoons of lemon juice into the bowl.

2. Add a few drops of water.

3. Dip the paintbrush into the lemon juice mixture and write a message on the paper. Wait for it to dry.

4. With help from an adult, carefully hold the paper close to a lit lightbulb until the paper feels warm and the message appears.

HARD-BOILED MESSAGE

In his book *Magia Naturalis* [Natural Magic], published in 1558, Italian scholar Giovanni Battista della Porta described a method for writing secret messages on hard-boiled eggs. He used a mixture of vinegar and the chemical compound alum to write a message on the eggshell that would disappear when it dried. The ink would seep through the semiporous shell, and when the egg was peeled, the secret message would be visible on the egg white!

NINJA WRITING

In 2019, Japanese student Eimi Haga wrote an essay about ninjas in invisible ink and was given a top grade for creativity. Using an old ninja technique called *aburidashi*, she spent hours soaking and crushing soybeans to make the ink. The words appeared when the teacher heated the paper over a gas stove.

WAX INK

The wax in a crayon repels water. As you paint over the white crayon message with the dark watercolor, you will see the message because the dark watercolor background won't stick to it.

YOU WILL NEED: white paper   medium-size paintbrush
white crayon   dark watercolor paint

1. Use the white crayon to write a message on the paper.

2. Use the paintbrush to paint over the message with the watercolor paint to make the message visible.

TABLE OF MEASURES

LENGTH/DISTANCE

1 foot = 12 inches

1 yard = 3 feet = 0.914 meter

1 meter = 39.37 inches

1 mile = 1,760 yards = 5,280 feet = 1.61 kilometers

1 kilometer = 0.62 mile

AREA

1 square inch = 6.45 square centimeters

1 square foot = 144 square inches

1 square yard = 9 square feet = 0.84 square meter

1 acre = 43,560 square feet = 0.40 hectare

1 hectare = 2.47 acres

1 square mile = 640 acres = 2.59 square kilometers

1 square kilometer = 0.386 square mile

HOUSEHOLD
(approx. equivalents)

½ teaspoon = 2.5 mL

1 teaspoon = 5 mL

3 teaspoons = 1 tablespoon = 15 mL

¼ cup = 60 mL

⅓ cup = 75 mL

½ cup = 120 mL

¾ cup = 175 mL

1 cup = 16 tablespoons = 8 ounces = 240 mL

2 liquid cups = 1 pint = 0.5 liter

2 liquid pints = 1 quart = 1 liter

4 liquid quarts = 1 gallon = 4 liters

SPEED/VELOCITY
(mph = miles per hour; kph = kilometers per hour)

1 mph = 1.609 kph

1 knot = 1.15 mph = 1.85 kph

COMPARE CELSIUS AND FAHRENHEIT

To convert Celsius and Fahrenheit

$$°C = (°F - 32) / 1.8 \quad \blacksquare \quad °F = (°C \times 1.8) + 32$$

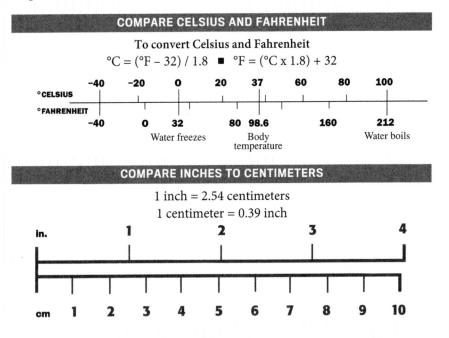

°CELSIUS	-40	-20	0	20	37	60	80	100
°FAHRENHEIT	-40	0	32	80	98.6		160	212

Water freezes   Body temperature   Water boils

COMPARE INCHES TO CENTIMETERS

1 inch = 2.54 centimeters

1 centimeter = 0.39 inch

in.   1   2   3   4

cm   1   2   3   4   5   6   7   8   9   10

"Penguin Puzzler" on page 49

"See the Bees" on page 73

"Color by Number" on page 89

"A Cheesy Maze" on page 133

"Find the Forest Dwellers" on page 165

"Sports Search" on page 143

ACKNOWLEDGMENTS

PICTURE CREDITS

ABBREVIATIONS:
FB–Facebook
GI–Getty Images
IGM–Instagram
**NASA–National Aeronautics and
        Space Administration**
SS–Shutterstock
WM–Wikimedia
WP–Wikipedia

Front Cover: Maryna Rayimova/GI
Back Cover: Team USA (Suni Lee). Zuzuzu/
WM (BTS). Bass Supakit/SS (leaf sheep).
Cylonphoto/GI (meteors). Ripley's Believe
It or Not! (brinicle). Kelly Alder (aliens).
PattayaPhotography/GI (piglets). Kharlamova/
GI (cartoon boy).
Calendar: 8: IGM (Carrie Ann Inaba).
WM (iPhone). St. Louis Zoo (rhinoceroses).
Britannica (Roberta Bondar). Tomdog/WM
(Adam Lambert). National Portrait Gallery,
Smithsonian Institution (Jackie Robinson).
9: Wirelmage (Shakira). Pinterest (Carly
Patterson). Joan Hernandez Mir/WM
(Michael B. Jordan). Harald Krichel/WM (Ed
Sheeran). National Park Service (Washington
Monument). Pixabay (strawberries).
10: Wirestock/GI (bird). Daniel Benavides/
WM (Lupita Nyong'o). Team USA (Suni Lee).
House of Hockey (Bobby Orr). NASA (John
Young). MaksimYremenko/GI (tornado).
11: Fredlyfish4/WM (Cannon Mountain).
Cosmopolitan UK/WM (Lil Nas X). NASA
(*Apollo 13*). Tidy Mom (peach cobbler).
Bright Star Musical (Beauty and the Beast).
Triplexace/WM (Dev Patel). writerfantast/
GI (cherry blossoms). 12: TatianaMironenko/
GI (flowers). Unicef/WM (David Beckham).
Ad Branch (Coca-Cola sign). Georges Biard/
WM (Rosario Dawson). Mingle Media TV/WM
(Tina Fey). Zuzuzu/WM (BTS). Disney/Lucas
Films (*Star Wars*). 13: Toglenn/WM (Heidi
Klum). Northfoto/SS (Prince). Hortimages/SS
(iced tea). Rita Molnár/WM (Nicole Kidman).
IGM (Vera Wang). Patrick Daxenbichler/GI
(flowers). 14: Rike_/GI (poppies). Britannica
(John A. Macdonald). upthebanner/GI (Statue
of Liberty). Twitter (Michelle Kwan). 5second/
GI (blueberry muffin). DalStars9/WM (Jamie
Benn). Earl McGehee/WM (Alison Krauss).
MTV International/WM (Sandra Bullock). NASA
(astronaut). 15: Skidmore/WM (Jason Momoa).
lightkitegirl/GI (watermelon). Raph_PH/WM
(Shawn Mendes). Supreme Court Historical
Society (Ruth Bader Ginsburg). IGM (Halle
Berry). mphillips007/GI (nachos). WCJB
(Martin Luther King Jr.). MilaDrumeva/GI
(butterflies). 16: Preto_perola/GI (leaves).
Toglenn/WM (Zendaya). Jeffhoffman2001/WM
(Mac Jones). Hershey (chocolate). Crayola
(crayons). Britannica (Jimmie Johnson).
Colombo Telegraph (John Lennon). 17: WM
(*Peanuts*). FB (Gwen Stefani). iDominick/WM
(Rowan Blanchard). Guggenheim.org
(Guggenheim Museum of Art). MTV
International/WM (Ryan Reynolds). Yulia
Melnyk/GI (chocolate). nitrub/GI (apples).
18: TShum/GI (berries in ice). Georges Biard/
WM (Emma Stone). Jedi94/WM (EPCOT).
IMDB (Pelé). Mihoko Yamamoto/GI (parfait).
Airman 1st Class Aleece Williams/WM
(Russell Wilson). 19: WM (Charlie Puth). WP
(*Le Bateau*). WP (Rudolph). eurobanks/GI
(brownies). Cosmopolitan UK/WM (Taylor
Swift). George Pimentel/IMDB (Maitreyi
Ramakrishnan). Kotenko_A/GI (winter sky).
20–21: Galina Timofeeva/GI (background, top).
Yurkina Alexandra/SS (illustrations).
20: Roman Mykhalchuk/GI (top left). McAndy/
GI (top right). Reimphoto/GI (center left).
fotogaby/GI (center right). Reimphoto/GI
(bottom left). Meyer & Meyer/GI (bottom right).
21: Arzakae/SS (top left). stock_colors/GI (top
right). Dan Olsen/GI (center left). William G
Forbes/SS (center right). Minakryn Ruslan/SS
(bottom left). ConradFries/GI (bottom right).
22: Vitalii Abakumov/GI (illustrations).
23: ImagineGolf/GI. 24: kenneth-cheung/GI
(top). Fawcett5/WP (bottom). 25: nico_blue/GI.
Astronomy: 26–29: Cylonphoto/GI.
30–35: Kelly Alder (illustrations). 36–41:

ACKNOWLEDGMENTS

Rob Schuster (illustrations).
Weather: 42: Leonid Ikan/SS (background). subjug/GI. 43: Alexandrum79/GI (top). Sycamore Land Trust (bottom). 44: saiko3p/GI (top). elmvilla/GI (center). staphy/GI (bottom). 45: steve_is_on_holiday/GI (top). LexussK/GI (center left). Ripley's Believe It or Not! (bottom). 46: Wasrts/WM (top). Vielfalt/WM (center right). News Spectrum 1 (center left). filmfoto/GI (bottom). 47: RBOZUK/GI (top right). Evolista (center right). Canadian Tire Corporation (bottom). 48: Felt Magic (top). helen vt/SS (bottom). 49: Ksenya Savva/SS. 50-51: Pavel G/SS. 52-55: Dubov/GI (background). 52: NASA (top). Marcel Bourgeois/Saltwire (center). 53: Roel Loopers Freo's View (top). yanik88/GI (center). choja/GI (bottom left). iso_petrov/GI (bottom right). 54: travelview/GI (top). National Oceanic Atmospheric Administration (center). alex5248/GI (bottom). 56: Greekmythology.com. 57: Crafts by Amanda (top left). Inner Child Fun (top right). Hands On As We Grow (bottom left). Sugar, Spice, and Glitter (bottom right).
In the Garden: 58: jamesbenet/GI (top left). Chepko/GI (top right). nechaev-kon/GI (center left). Pacotoscano/GI (center right). marcouliana/GI (bottom left). sbonk/GI (bottom right). GoodStudio/SS (illustration). 59: Konstantin Shashkov/GI (top left). CathyKeifer/GI (top right). Acoll123/GI (bottom left). marcophotos/GI (bottom right). 60: jamesbenet/GI (top). nechaev-kon/GI (center). CathyKeifer/GI (bottom). GoodStudio/SS (illustration). 61: Pacotoscano/GI (top). Chepko/GI (center right). Acoll123/GI (bottom left). Konstantin Shashkov/GI (bottom right). GoodStudio/SS (illustration). 62: marcouliana/GI (top left). Oleg Marchak/GI (top right). sbonk/GI (bottom left). Marshall Grain Co. (bottom middle). marcophotos/GI (bottom right). GoodStudio/SS (illustration). 63: fotolinchen/GI (top, yarrow). GettyTim82/GI (top, goldenrod). Etsy (bottom). GoodStudio/SS (illustration). 64-65: BNP Design Studio/SS. 66: Sherwood Seeds (top). Bonnie Plants (center). bergamont/GI (bottom). 67: Hudson Valley Seed Company (top). Trade Winds Fruit (center). Amazon (bottom). 68: Grow Organic (top left). Gardens Alive (top right). ThomasLENNE/SS (bottom). 69: Eden Brothers (top). bhofack2/GI (bottom left). Burpee (bottom right). 70: Bogdan Lazar/GI (top). marcouliana/GI (bottom). 71: WM (top). Cerise HUA/GI (center). PeaceLilyPhotography/GI (bottom). 72: Pinterest (top). Andreas Häuslbetz/GI (center). 73: Lexi Claus/SS. 74-75: paul_june/GI (border). Photonaj/GI (tulips). Alexandrum79/GI (sunflowers). allou/GI (hydrangeas). brainstorm1962/GI (dahlias).
On the Farm: 76-77: anopdesignstock/GI. 78-81: Gabriel Onat/GI (background). 78: graphic-bee/GI (top). *Des Moines Register* (center). iiievgeniy/GI (bottom). 79: wakila/GI (top). Dr. Candace Croney (center). graphic-bee/GI (bottom). 80: Guinness World Records (top left). graphic-bee/GI (top right). Tinseltown/SS (center left). fandom.com (center right). peppapig.com (bottom). 81: graphic-bee/GI (top). PattayaPhotography/GI (bottom). 82-83: Chanakarn/GI (speech bubbles). CandO_Designs/GI (pigs). Dualororua/SS (donkeys). pepan/SS (horses). 82: ONYXprj/GI (bees and hive). Memo Angeles/SS (goats). 83: ONYXprj/GI (cows). Memo Angeles/SS (chickens). ONYXprj/GI (sheep). 84-85: egal/GI. 84: Kontrec/GI. 86: virgonira/GI (top). CreativeNature_nl/GI (center). miflippo/GI (bottom). 87: dvdwinters/GI (top). Christos Georghiou/SS (center). 89: Lexi Claus/SS.
Nature: 90-91: Maryna Rayimova/GI. 92-97: klerik78/GI (background). 92: AGAMI stock/GI (top). KenCanning/GI (center). Uwe-Bergwitz/GI (bottom). 93: pixcolo/GI (top). ohnpane/GI (center). gatito33/GI (bottom). 94: MriyaWildlife/GI (top). DmitryND/GI (bottom). 95: Tyrannax/GI (top). mtnmichelle/GI (center). moose henderson/GI (bottom). 96: dschaef/GI (top). Rusmwood/GI (center). Rejean Bedard/GI (bottom). 97: sduben/GI (top right). Maximilien Leblanc/GI (top left). Kim Marriott/SS (center). Warren Howe/GI (bottom left). MajaPhoto/GI (bottom right). 98: Paul Hartley/GI (top). Janet Griffin-Scott/GI (bottom left). M. Leonard Photography/GI (bottom right). 99: bookguy/GI (top). camacho9999/GI (bottom). 100: ps50ace/GI. 101: KenCanning/GI. 102: InsectWorld/SS. 103: Bass Supakit/

SS. 104: Jay Ondreicka/SS. 105: ratselmeister/ SS. 106–107: MargaretW/GI. 108–109: Sean Pavone/GI (background). 108: Appalachian Trail Conservancy (top left, center, bottom middle). AMC Library and Archive (top right). Dartmouth Library (bottom left). 109: Appalachian Trail Conservancy (top left). Josh Sutton (top right). llusmaa.org (center). International Appalachian Trail (bottom right). 110–111: Jon Bilous/GI (background). 110: NetaDegany/GI. 111: Courtesy of Eddie Lough. **Awesome Achievers:** 112: Chelsea's Charity/FB. 114: GoFundMe. 115: FB. 116: IGM. 117: Black-Owned Businesses. 118–122: saenal78/GI (background). 118: Guinness World Records. 119: Twitter. 120: NeilNayyar .com. 121: NME/GI. 122: Bluegrass Today. 123: Alena Razumova/SS. **Food:** 124: Midget Momma. 126–127: Cook Shoots Food/GI. 127: Yulia Melnyk/GI. 128: gvardgraph/GI (top). xamtiw/GI (ricotta). Iuliia Kanivets/GI (protein bar). 129: andegro4ka/GI (top right, all). Yulia Melnyk/GI (bottom left). BWFolsom/GI (bottom right). 130: PanNguyen/ GI (top). Floortje/GI (center). kajakiki/GI (bottom). 131: bhofack2/GI (top). subjug/GI (center left). Yulia Melnyk/GI (center right). P Kyriakos/SS (bottom). 132: AlexPro9500/ GI. 133: Vector Tradition/SS. 134: katyau/ GI (background). The Kahimyang Project. 135: Allen Gabriel Cruz. 136–137: katyau/GI (background). 137: Cara Cormack/The Spruce. **Sports:** 138: jonah_H/GI. 139: Ryan McVay/GI (top). artisteer/GI (center). Dmytro Aksonov/ GI (bottom). 140: francisblack/GI. 141: hhof/ Hockey News (bottom left). eBay (bottom middle). GerryCheeevers.com (bottom right). 142: BonoMac/GI (left). Glenn Hall/Websports (right). 143: chaweekun/SS. 144–147: Tim Robinson (illustrations). **Health:** 148–151: Tim Robinson (illustrations). 152–153: amino/SS (background). calvindexter/GI (all). **Amusement:** 154: chuteye/SS (all). 156: Kyrychenko Anastasiia/SS (top). Jupiterimages/ GI (center left). alaik/GI (bottom). 157: Victor_ Brave/GI (center right). NASA (Neil Armstrong). Raph_PH/WM (Lady Gaga). Pete Souza/ Official White House Photo (Barack Obama).

Lorie Shaull/WM (A'ja Wilson). 158–159: Renee Dobbs/spoiledhounds.com. 160: Sarah Bond/ BoneAppetreat.com. 161: Jen Wooster-McBride/peelwithzeal.com. 162–164: Tim Robinson (illustrations). 165: Kharlamova/ GI. 166–169: Zaksheuskaya/SS (background). 166: British Library (bottom). 167: Research Parent. 168: This West Coast Mommy (top). 169: *Daily Mail* (top). Artful Parent (bottom). 171: Ksenya Savva/SS (top left). Lexi Claus/SS (top right). Lexi Claus/SS (center left). Vector Tradition/SS (center right). chaweekun/SS (bottom left). Kharlamova/GI (bottom right).

CONTRIBUTORS

Mel Allen: The Toughest Job in Sports. **Bob Berman:** 8 Tips for Watching the Geminid Meteor Shower. **Catherine Boeckmann:** What Flower Are You? **Sarah Bond:** Pops for Your Pup. **Alice Cary:** Go Take a Hike—On the Appalachian Trail!; Changing the World, One Kid at a Time; Music Marvels; María Orosa's Edible Inventions; When Left Is Right. **Renee Dobbs:** Pops for Your Pup. **Tim Goodwin:** Birthday Bling, A Day to Honor Indigenous Peoples, UFOs: Fact or Fiction?, Ice Time, Hay! Is That Straw?, Anyone for Frisbeener? **Mare-Anne Jarvela:** Follow the Rainbow of Vegetables, This Little Piggy, Say "Cheeeeeeeese"!, Undercover Ink. **Rosemary Mosco:** The Great Night Flight. **Sheryl Normandeau:** Creature Corner. **Sarah Perreault:** What Happened in History?, Incredible Ice Cream Bread, Unwind Your Mind, Brain Freeze! **Jack Singal:** Does Outer Space End? (reprinted with permission from **The Conversation,** theconversation. com). **Heidi Stonehill:** Sly as a Fox. **Robin Sweetser:** Beneficial Bugs. **Jen Wooster-McBride:** Pops for Your Pup.

Content not cited here is adapted from *The Old Farmer's Almanac* archives or appears in the public domain. Every effort has been made to attribute all material correctly. If any errors have been unwittingly committed, they will be corrected in a future edition.

INDEX

ACTIVITIES